Traditional African American Arts and Activities

CELEBRATING OUR HERITAGE

Traditional African American Arts and Activities

Sonya Kimble-Ellis

John Wiley & Sons, Inc.

For the wonderful children in my family (cousins, nieces, and nephews), this is for you.
In loving memory of Kyle J. Bennett.

Published by John Wiley & Sons, Inc., New York
Published simultaneously in Canada

Illustrations by Gary Estime

Design and production by Navta Associates, Inc.

The publisher and the author have made every reasonable effort to ensure that the experiments and activities in the book are safe when conducted as instructed but assume no responsibility for any damage caused or sustained while performing the experiments or activities in this book. Parents, guardians, and/or teachers should supervise young readers who undertake the experiments and activities in this book.

Library of Congress Cataloging-in-Publication Data:

Kimble-Ellis, Sonya.
    Traditional African American arts and activities / Sonya Kimble-Ellis.
        p. cm.—(Celebrating our heritage)
    Includes index.
    Contents: Celebrations—Traditions—Crafts—Games—Culture—Soul and Caribbean foods.
    Summary: A collection of activities focusing on cultural traditions related to African American history, including celebrations like Kwanzaa and Juneteenth, activities such as storytelling and hair braiding, and games such as Mancala.
    ISBN 0-471-41046-2 (acid-free paper)
      1. African Americans—Social life and customs—Juvenile literature. 2. African American arts—Juvenile literature. 3. African Americans—Social life and customs—Study and teaching (Elementary)—Activity programs—Juvenile literature. 4. African American arts—Study and teaching (Elementary)—Activity programs—Juvenile literature. [1. African Americans—Social life and customs. 2. African American arts. 3. Handicraft.] I. Title. II. Series.

E185.86 .K56 2002   2001046545
394'.089'96073—dc21

Printed in the United States of America

10 9 8 7 6 5 4 3 2 1

Contents

Acknowledgments   vii

Introduction   1

I. Celebrations   3
Martin Luther King Jr. Day   5
Black History Month   10
Juneteenth   14
Kwanzaa   18

II. Traditions   23
Storytelling and Folktales   25
Hair Braiding   30
Quilting   35

III. Crafts   41
Calabash   43
Adire (Tie-Dyeing)   46
Mask Making   50
Drums   54

IV. Games   59
Mancala   61
Little Sally Walker   64
Muraburaba   66
Chigoro Danda   69

V. Culture   73
Music   75
   Blues, Gospel, and Soul   *76*
   Jazz   *81*
   Rap   *84*
Dance   87
   Contemporary and Ballet Dancing   *88*
   Tap   *92*
Literature   95

VI. Soul Food and Caribbean Cuisine   101
Corn Bread and Biscuits   103
Fried Plantain   107

Glossary   109

Index   113

Acknowledgments

A special thanks to those whose help and support made the completion of this book possible: my husband Michael for his patience, understanding, and help with the initial sketches for this book; Lynda Jones for her generosity and friendship in referring me for this project; my mother, Dolores Kimble, and Aunt Jackie for help with the recipes; Aunt Barbara, I didn't forget you this time; Thelma and Glenda Mattox for their time and invaluable information for the section on quilting; the research staffs at the Schomburg Center for Culture and Research, the Newark Public Library, and Maplewood Memorial Library for all their assistance; Tri Ba and Beresford Ellis for answering my hair, craft, and Caribbean food questions, respectively; Antoinette Ellis-Williams for the recipe suggestion; the Smith family, especially Debbie, for the support that means so much to me; a special thanks to all my other family members; and to my editor, Kate Bradford, and the Wiley staff for your assistance and for making this project a reality.

Introduction

As my editor would certainly agree, deciding what activities and information should be included in this book was a challenging task. It was one, though, that I welcomed with open arms. One issue that came up early on was choosing activities and crafts that were thought of as exclusively African American. That presented a problem because many of the crafts and games African Americans embrace today are African in origin. They weren't developed by African Americans who lived in the United States.

Because African Americans lost much of their culture during slavery, two important outcomes resulted. The last several hundred years have been spent developing the African American culture (dance, music, celebrations, etc.) we enjoy today; and a continual effort is made (especially today) to embrace the African culture that was lost. That is why many African Americans embrace purely African traditions and games. You will read about many of them here in this text.

One important note to make is that several time periods in history are discussed throughout this book. Historically, African Americans have been identified by a number of different names, including *colored, negro,* and *black.* The term African American is the one that will be used most frequently here.

In addition to the fun activities in this book, it is my hope that the information within these chapters provides valuable history lessons on African American culture, traditions, ancestry, creativity, and foods. Enjoy!

I CELEBRATIONS

For centuries, celebrations have been an important part of African American culture. While some celebrations are historical and honor African American accomplishments and contributions, others—such as family reunions, holidays, and church revivals—recognize cultural or religious traditions. The rituals associated with these celebrations vary. Events are honored with feasts, festivals, fairs, ceremonies, or parades.

In the 1700s, several African American celebrations were called **hallowdays** (elections and coronations observed by free African Americans and slaves living in the North). These activities copied those of whites in New England who allowed their slaves to attend their election festivities for new governors. By the mid-1700s, African Americans were having their own elections where they selected a governor or a king. The person chosen was usually someone who had been born in Africa and was known to come from African royalty.

The African American coronation festivities also duplicated the actions of the slave owners. Usually, the newly elected African American governor was the slave of the best-known and richest master. And because the slave master had a great deal of money, the slaves would try to convince him to sponsor grand festivals (similar to the ones held by whites) which included food, drink, dancing, and music. More than just hold a title, the African American governor acted as a counselor to slaves who had difficulty with their slave masters.

In modern times, African American celebrations such as Martin Luther King Jr. Day, Black History Month, Juneteenth, and Kwanzaa provide the opportunity to remember ancestry and history. They are a time to reflect on the struggles and social, political, and artistic contributions of African Americans who were born during an earlier period. And finally, these celebrations help unite people in communities, strengthen families, and reinforce the traditions African Americans embrace every day.

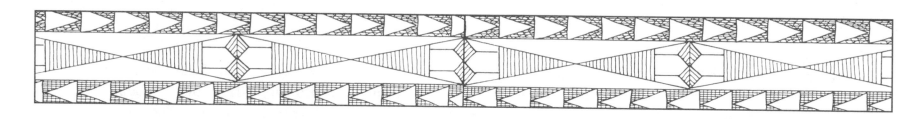

Martin Luther King Jr. Day

Martin Luther King Jr. © *Bettmann/CC*

"So I say to you, my friends, that even though we must face the difficulties of today and tomorrow, I still have a dream. It is a dream deeply rooted in the American dream that one day this nation will rise up and live out the true meaning of its creed. . . . We hold these truths to be self-evident, that all men are created equal."

DR. MARTIN LUTHER KING JR.

Martin Luther King Jr. was the third person in American history to be honored with a national holiday. The road to making his birthday a national holiday, however, was almost as challenging as many of his **civil rights** (the rights of citizens to equality and political and social freedom) efforts.

The son of a Baptist preacher, King was born in 1929 in Atlanta, Georgia. As a young man, he was encouraged by his family to follow in his father's footsteps. During his teens, King was unsure about the kind of work he wanted to pursue. But while attending Morehouse College in Atlanta, he was convinced by the school's president that he could use Christianity as a way to improve things in society. He then went on to study theology at Boston University and soon began giving sermons at local churches and at his father's church in Atlanta.

Throughout his life, Dr. King fought for equality among the races. His goal was to achieve equality through nonviolent protests, marches, and boycotts. His quest started in 1955, when an African American woman named Rosa Parks was arrested in Montgomery, Alabama for refusing to give up her seat on a bus to a white passenger. Soon after the incident, King was asked to be the president of the Montgomery Improvement Association, an organization developed to organize a boycott of Montgomery buses. As part of the boycott, hundreds of blacks refused to ride the buses for months. Local bus companies lost a lot of money and a message was sent to the rest of the country that blacks had the power to protest unfair treatment. In 1956, the U.S. Supreme Court declared bus segregation unconstitutional.

King continued to protest other unfair practices by joining students in Atlanta, Georgia in 1960 to participate in "lunch-counter sit-ins." Their fight for the right to be served food in white restaurants was eventually won. In 1963, he found himself in Birmingham, Alabama, challenging the fact that black and white students had to attend separate schools. Because of the efforts of King and others in the Civil Rights movement, President John F. Kennedy introduced a Civil Rights Bill that led to the **desegregation** (abolition of racial segregation) of all U.S. schools.

On August 28, 1963, more than 200,000 people attended a march on Washington. They gathered to protest the unfair treatment of African Americans in voting and housing. During the event, King delivered his famous "I Have a Dream" speech. His words passionately expressed his thoughts and feelings about equality and are remembered by millions.

On March 7, 1965, King led a demonstration from Selma, Alabama to the State Capitol in Montgomery. He and other demonstrators were asking for the right of African Americans to vote in local and national elections. Upon Governor George Wallace's orders, marchers were attacked with dogs, clubs, and tear gas in an effort to stop the march. The outbreak was seen on television and caused the nation to realize the severity of the Civil Rights problem and the need to do something to solve it. Due to

MAKING THE HOLIDAY

The King Holiday campaign was started by Michigan Congressman John Conyers four days after King was assassinated in 1968. It took some time for the legislation to gain total support. There were many people who felt there were other Americans who deserved to have their birthdays declared a holiday before King. But supporters of the King holiday moved ahead with their plans.

Over the next few decades, many people supported the passing of the King Holiday bill. In 1983, Coretta Scott King, musician Stevie Wonder, and the Reverend Jesse Jackson led a march to Washington, D.C., to encourage Congress to pass the bill. Wonder even recorded a song called "Happy Birthday" in honor of King's birthday. President Ronald Reagan made Martin Luther King Jr. Day a federal holiday in 1986.

King's efforts and public pressure, President Lyndon B. Johnson signed the Voting Rights Act of 1965, which gave blacks the right to vote.

King also spoke out on the Vietnam War, poverty, and equal employment opportunities. He was awarded the Nobel Peace Prize in 1964 for his nonviolent Civil Rights accomplishments. In 1968, he was shot and killed while standing on a hotel balcony in Memphis, Tennessee. Although James Earl Ray was convicted of the crime, people still wonder if someone else may have killed Dr. King. A year after his death, King's wife, Coretta Scott King, opened the Martin Luther King Jr. Center for Nonviolent Social Change in Atlanta. She and Martin Luther King Jr.'s four children, Yolanda, Martin Luther III, Dexter, and Denise, continue to carry on his legacy.

King's birthday, which is January 15, is celebrated on the third Monday in January. Because it is a national holiday, post offices, schools, federal offices, and banks are closed. African Americans in particular celebrate the holiday with speeches and panel discussions about King's contributions, and with concerts, dances and choral performances that honor his life. Today, all fifty states honor King's birthday. It is also celebrated in many countries around the world.

Martin Luther King Jr. contributed a great deal to American history through his accomplishments in the fight for African American civil rights. Make your own MLK scroll to commemorate his contributions.

Martin Luther King Jr. Scroll

Here's What You Need

- 2 pieces of tubular cardboard from clothes hangers (Most dry cleaners have hangers with tubular cardboard that are usually used for hanging pants and skirts.)
- ruler
- pen
- scissors
- newspaper
- colored markers
- piece of 10-by-16-inch (25-by-41-cm) construction paper (any color)
- stapler
- wool yarn

Here's What You Do

1 Remove the cardboard tubes from the hangers. Using your ruler, measure 12 inches (30 cm) along each piece of cardboard. Use a pen to mark the spot. Cut each piece of cardboard where you drew the mark so that you now have two 12-inch (30-cm)–long tubes. Discard the smaller pieces of cardboard.

2 Lay a large piece of newspaper on the floor or on a table. Place the cardboard tubes on the newspaper. Use colored markers to completely cover the tubes, from one end to the other, with your own design. Allow at least 15 minutes for your marker drawings to dry.

3 Place one short edge of the piece of construction paper along one of the tubes, centering it in the middle. Using a stapler that is opened to a tacking position, staple the construction paper to the tube. Staple the opposite edge of your construction paper to the other tube. This is your scroll.

8 CELEBRATIONS

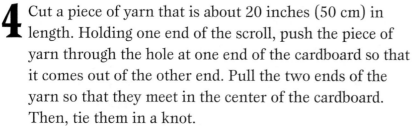

4 Cut a piece of yarn that is about 20 inches (50 cm) in length. Holding one end of the scroll, push the piece of yarn through the hole at one end of the cardboard so that it comes out of the other end. Pull the two ends of the yarn so that they meet in the center of the cardboard. Then, tie them in a knot.

5 At the top of your scroll, draw a picture of Dr. King or make a copy from a book or magazine, then write his name underneath. Use the rest of your scroll to write an essay about why you admire King, list the 10 things you admire most about him, or write a poem. Now hang your Martin Luther King Jr. scroll on your bedroom wall.

To learn more about Dr. King, read one of the following books:

America in the King Years by Taylor Branch
Martin Luther King: Man with a Dream by Jon Davidoff
Why We Can't Wait by Martin Luther King Jr.
The Measure of a Man by Martin Luther King Jr.

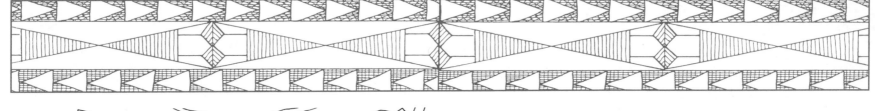

Black History Month

> *[Black History Month is] now a celebration that's found in the smallest villages in America, as well as in the largest urban centers.*
>
> DR. MOLEFI KETE ASANTE

Many people know that Harriet Tubman escorted hundreds of slaves to freedom through the Underground Railroad and that Madam C. J. Walker was the first African American female millionaire. But did you know that the railway signal was invented by A. B. Blackburn or that Garrett A. Morgan invented the gas mask? They were both African American inventors.

Little-known facts like these are part of the reason historian Carter G. Woodson started Negro History Week in 1926. Black history was largely ignored in American history books and classes during that time. Woodson thought it was important that African Americans, as well as people of all races, recognize African American culture, accomplishments, contributions to the arts, and history.

What Woodson didn't know at the time was that nearly forty-five years later, his seven-day remembrance would become a vibrant monthlong celebration. Today, Black History Month, which takes place in February, is one of the most diverse African American celebrations. People across the country honor and explore African American history with lectures, fairs, festivals, concerts, seminars, dance recitals, and plays.

Woodson chose the second week of February, in honor of Frederick Douglass's birthday, for the celebration. He then sent out pamphlets to schools, churches, civic associations, newspapers, women's clubs, and state boards of education around the country to suggest ways people could celebrate. He created Negro History Week kits, posters, and photographs that he later sold. Woodson also sold a listing called "152 Important Events and Dates in Negro History."

Teachers played a big role in the development and growth of Negro History Week. They came up with fun and exciting ways for students to celebrate the holiday, and some even created Negro History Week study clubs. These clubs devoted an entire school year to studying blacks in America. Outside of school, Negro History Week was celebrated with poetry readings, exhibitions, banquets, speeches, and parades featuring people dressed as famous African Americans.

Carter G. Woodson died in 1950. But by 1970, the Association for the Study of Negro Life and History, an organization Woodson founded, decided the celebration should last a month. They also replaced the word *Negro* with *Black*.

Today, Black History Month is recognized in every state with events ranging from film festivals and television specials to community arts and heritage celebrations. Families, organizations, libraries, museums, schools, and cultural centers all take part in this annual celebration, which is a time to reflect on the contributions of African Americans, their culture, and their history.

Create a Black History Month banner by stringing together images that represent important moments and events in African American history.

Black History Month Banner

Here's What You Need

- ☐ pencil
- ☐ 3 or more pieces of construction paper (any color)
- ☐ Styrofoam cup
- ☐ scissors
- ☐ one-hole paper punch
- ☐ ruler
- ☐ knitting yarn

Here's What You Do

1 Draw your first black history item, a bus, on one of the pieces of construction paper. The bus represents the Montgomery bus boycott, the first major Civil Rights event, which took place in 1955. Use the bottom of the cup as a guide to draw the wheels. Using your pencil, trace the cup to draw the first wheel. Draw the rest of the bus around the wheels. Cut the bus out of the piece of construction paper.

2 The mailbox was invented in 1891 by African American inventor P. B. Downing. Draw your own mailbox on another piece of construction paper. Cut out the drawing.

3 Make more cutouts that represent moments in African American history. Another cutout you can add to your banner is a school to represent the fight for school desegregation.

4 Lay all of your cutouts on a table. Using a paper punch, punch a hole in each end of the top of each cutout. Cut four 8-inch (20-cm) pieces of yarn. Connect each cutout by threading a piece of yarn through each hole and tying a knot. Attach the yarn to your wall with nails so that the banner hangs across your room. You can make your Black History Month banner longer by drawing images that represent other black history events, accomplishments, or inventions by African Americans.

BLACK HISTORY NOTE

On May 17, 1954, the U.S. Supreme Court ruled unanimously that racial segregation in public schools in America was unconstitutional. Three years later, nine African American high school students in Little Rock, Arkansas, were escorted to school by federal troops.

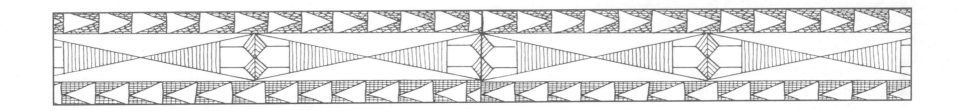

Juneteenth

"The people of Texas are informed that in accordance with a Proclamation from the Executive of the United States, all slaves are free. This involves an absolute equality of rights and rights of property between former masters and slaves, and the connection heretofore existing between them becomes that between employer and free laborer.

GENERAL GORDON GRANGER
GALVESTON, TEXAS

Juneteenth commemorates the date that slaves in Texas were told slavery had ended. Although President Lincoln's Emancipation Proclamation freed the slaves on January 1, 1863, slaves in Texas didn't hear the news until June 19, 1865. It was delivered by General Gordon Granger and Union soldiers. Rumor has it that the news of the **emancipation** (freedom from slavery) was deliberately withheld by slave masters so that they could keep slaves working on their plantations. Others say federal troops waited until another crop season passed before they spread the word of freedom. When slaves in Texas finally did hear the news, there was cause for great celebration.

The slaves gave that famous day the name Juneteenth, which is a combination of the words *June* and *Nineteenth*. The oldest celebration honoring the end of slavery, Juneteenth originated in Galveston, Texas. The celebrations were, and still are, a major event in many states across the country, especially Minnesota, Wisconsin, and Texas. Picnics and food have always been a big part of the celebrations, with people preparing dishes that included pork, lamb, and beef. Barbecuing is a popular Juneteenth tradition that allows African Americans to connect with the way their newly freed ancestors must have felt during their celebrations. Because of this, barbecue pits and grills are a centerpiece at most Juneteenth celebrations. In addition to barbecuing, participants enjoy drinking red or strawberry soda, creating music with handmade instruments, singing, and sharing stories with friends and family. Other typical activities include fishing and rodeos.

During slavery, most slaves were told what they could and couldn't wear. In the early Juneteenth celebrations, slaves threw their clothing into the river and took the newer clothes of their former masters to wear. This ritual symbolized a new beginning. Today, sharing stories about ancestors is an important part of Juneteenth celebrations. Prayer, self-education, and self-improvement activities are also important.

REDISCOVERING JUNETEENTH

During the early 1900s, Juneteenth celebrations were few. As former slaves began to move to the North and found jobs, they were unable to celebrate the day unless it fell on a Saturday or Sunday. People also found it difficult to continue Juneteenth celebrations because the emancipation of slaves was officially recognized as having taken place in January of 1863. African Americans rediscovered Juneteenth during the Civil Rights era and more people began celebrating the date.

Today, Juneteenth is celebrated in a number of states. In addition to local citizen celebrations, annual Juneteenth activities are sponsored by the Henry Ford Museum in Dearborn, Michigan, and the Smithsonian Institution in Washington, D.C. On January 1, 1980, Legislator Al Edwards was successful in getting a bill passed in Texas that made Juneteenth an official state holiday.

Many Juneteenth activities took place outdoors, near rivers and creeks. Former slaves made baskets from pine and other trees, using them to carry their food and clothing to the picnic site. Make your own basket from colored cardboard.

Juneteenth Picnic Basket

Here's What You Need

- pencil
- ruler
- 2 different colored large sheets of cardboard at least 29½ by 13 inches (75 by 33 cm)
- scissors
- masking tape
- glue

Here's What You Do

1 Use the pencil and ruler to mark eight 1½-by-23-inch (4-by-60-cm) strips on one sheet of cardboard. Cut out the strips. Mark the strips 8½ inches (22 cm) from each end.

2 Mark three 1½-by-29½-inch (4-by-75-cm) strips on the second sheet of cardboard. Cut out these strips.

3 Lay four of the shorter strips next to each other on a table. Use masking tape to tape the ends together. Weave the fifth short strip in and out between the four strips. Take the three remaining short strips and weave them through the four strips in an alternating pattern as shown. Gently push the woven strips together in the middle of the original four strips, using the marks as a guide. Make sure all of the ends of the woven strips are even. Carefully remove the tape.

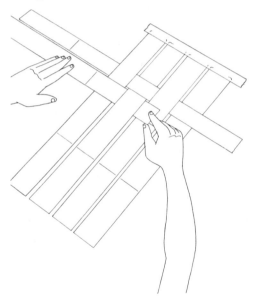

4 Bend the strips that make up the four sides upward at the marks to make a basket shape. Weave the first long strip around the bottom edge of the basket, bending the strip at each corner. Overlap the ends of the strip on the inside of the basket. Weave the two remaining long strips around the basket, keeping each one close to the strip that went before.

Cut two strips of the same size in the other cardboard color. Lay the strips flat so that they overlap with about half of each strip showing, then glue them together. When the glue has dried, glue each end of the handle to the inside of the basket.

5 To complete the top of the basket, bend the free end of each short strip over the top long strip. Alternate bending one end inside the basket and the next end outside the basket as shown. Continue this pattern all the way around the basket. Now glue all the ends down.

6 To make the handle, cut one strip of colored cardboard that measures 16¹⁄₂ by ³⁄₄ inches (42 by 2 cm).

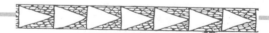

Juneteenth Tradition

During the late 1800s, many former slaves and their descendants made an annual **pilgrimage** (a journey taken for sentimental reasons) to Galveston on June 19 to celebrate the emancipation of Texas slaves.

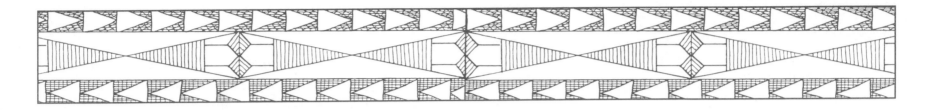

Kwanzaa

"*The principles of Kwanzaa are what African Americans needed in order to rebuild and strengthen family, community, and culture and become a self-conscious social force in the struggle to control their destiny and daily life.*"

MAULANA RON KARENGA

Kwanzaa (which means "first fruits") is known as the first African American cultural celebration. Created in 1966 by Professor Maulana Ron Karenga, this seven-day holiday is a time for family members to become closer. African Americans are also encouraged to take this time to recognize African culture and influences, and to honor the seven principles of Kwanzaa, which are called the **Nguzo Saba.**

THE PRINCIPLES OF KWANZAA

Here are the Nguzo Saba listed by their Swahili names. Each Swahili name is followed by the English translation of the word and its cultural meaning.

Umoja (u-mo-ja): Unity—to build togetherness as a family, community, and nation.

Kujichagulia (ku-jee-cha-gu-lee-a): Self-Determination—to work toward doing things that will strengthen your future.

Ujima (u-jee-ma): Collective Work and Responsibility—to work together and to help others.

Ujama (u-ja-ma): Cooperative Economics —to develop jobs and businesses that benefit your family and the community.

Nia (nee-a): Purpose—to work with others to make life better.

Kuumba (kuum-ba): Creativity—to use your talents to uplift others.

Imani (ee-ma-nee): Faith—to believe in God, yourself, your family, and others.

Kwanzaa is celebrated annually in the United States from December 26 through January 1 with traditional soul food dishes such as sweet potato pie, collard greens, and chicken, and Kwanzaa gifts and symbols that are used to decorate the home. At the start of the festivities, a straw mat called a **mkeka** (m-kay-ca) is placed on a table. On the mat are placed the **kikombe cha umoja** (kee-com-bay cha oo-mo-jah), a symbolic cup that is also known as the **unity cup;** a **Muhindi** (moo-heen-dee), an ear of corn to represent each child in the family; and various fruits and vegetables (such as grapes, bananas, and greens), called **mazao** (ma-zao), to represent the harvest and symbolize of the importance of working together.

The **kinara** (kee-naa-rah) is a wooden candleholder that is placed in the center of the table. Seven candles, called **mishumma** (mee-shoo-maah), represent the seven days and principles of Kwanzaa. One black candle is in the center of the candleholder, three red candles are on the left, and three green candles are on the right. The colors represent the red, black, and green flag that was often carried by Marcus Garvey, a black leader born in Jamaica. Red represents the blood of African people; black is for the faces of Africans; and green is for the hope and prosperity of Africa. Starting with the black candle, a different candle is lit each day in honor of a principle.

Karamu (ka-ra-moo) is a special feast held on December 31 or January 1. During the feast, families eat a big meal, tell stories, and discuss how they plan to apply the seven principles in the upcoming year. Also during the feast, the oldest family member pours juice into the unity cup, which represents togetherness, and everyone drinks from it. In doing so, they honor the eldest family member. When family members drink from the unity cup, they say, "Harambee!" (ha-rahm-bee), which means "to pull together."

Zawadi (za-wah-dee), symbolizing acts of kindness and caring, are gifts made for family and friends. Zawadi often include handmade beaded necklaces and bracelets, or crafts and books related to African or African American culture.

Professor Karenga started Kwanzaa and developed its seven principles as a way to strengthen and rebuild the family. He got the idea for Kwanzaa in the 1960s when many African Americans were strongly embracing African language, dress, and culture. Kwanzaa is based on ceremonies held in various parts of Africa to commemorate the start of the harvest season ("first fruits"). During this time, farmers gave thanks for the food they grew. People in the village thanked the farmers and acknowledged the many gifts of nature. Depending on the tribe, the festivities might last from three to nine days.

To celebrate Kwanzaa this year, start by making a Kwanzaa necklace, a gift you can give to a family member or friend.

KWANZAA TRADITION

Throughout Kwanzaa, family and friends greet each other with the Swahili phrase "Habari gani" (ha-ba-ree gah-nee), which means "What's happening?" or "What's the news?"

Kwanzaa Necklace

Here's What You Need

- [ ] newspaper
- [ ] box of macaroni noodles
- [ ] water-based paints
- [ ] small paintbrush
- [ ] string or thread
- [ ] scissors
- [ ] transparent tape

Here's What You Do

1 Cover a table with several pieces of newspaper. Pour 36 noodles onto the newspaper, then separate them into three piles. Each pile should have 12 noodles.

2 Paint the noodles in one pile red. Paint the second pile of noodles black and the third pile green. Allow the paint to dry.

3 Cut a piece of string 24 inches (61 cm) long. Tape one end of the string onto the newspaper. Holding the free end of the string, thread the noodles to the string. As you thread, alternate the colors of the noodles, threading first a red, then a black, and then a green noodle.

4 Lift the taped end of the string from the newspaper. Tie the ends of the string together, making a double knot to secure the necklace. Give the Kwanzaa noodle necklace to a family member or friend.

II
TRADITIONS

African American traditions, whose origins date back thousands of years to the continent of Africa, call upon the imagination, life experiences, creativity, and the use of very little to make a lot. These customs have been passed down from parents to their children, and then on to their children's children.

One of the most popular and oldest of African American traditions is storytelling. Storytelling was very important in all African cultures long before any stories were written down. When Africans came to America as slaves, they continued the tradition and gave it an African American flair that reflected their experiences. Many of the stories told by ancestors were probably the basis for many popular African American books written in the twentieth century.

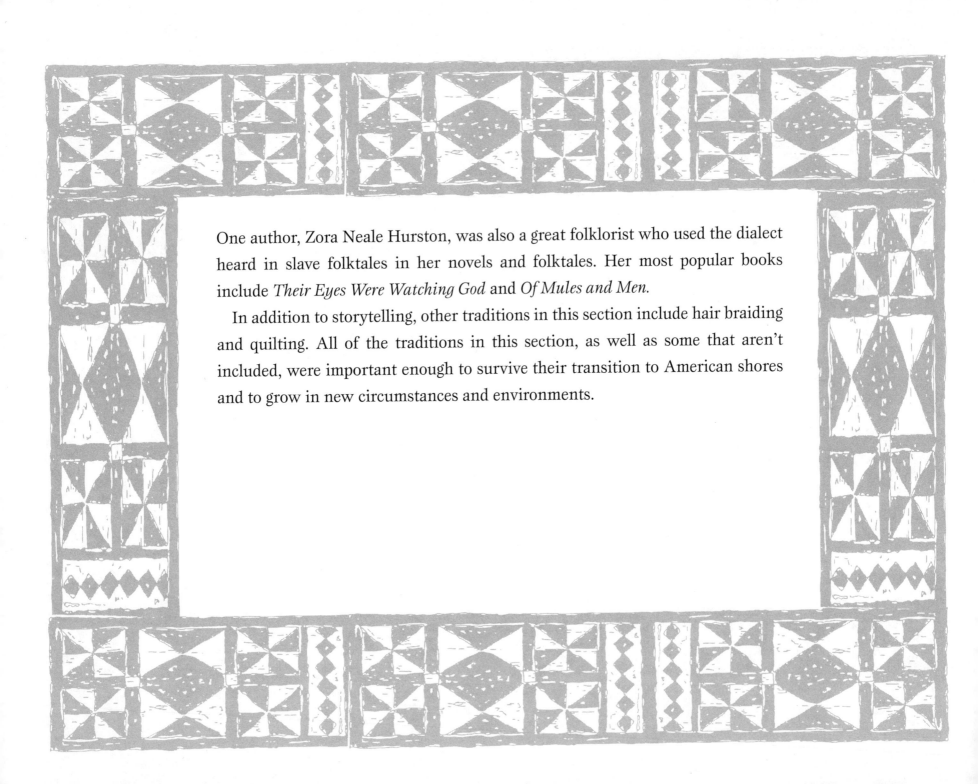

One author, Zora Neale Hurston, was also a great folklorist who used the dialect heard in slave folktales in her novels and folktales. Her most popular books include *Their Eyes Were Watching God* and *Of Mules and Men.*

In addition to storytelling, other traditions in this section include hair braiding and quilting. All of the traditions in this section, as well as some that aren't included, were important enough to survive their transition to American shores and to grow in new circumstances and environments.

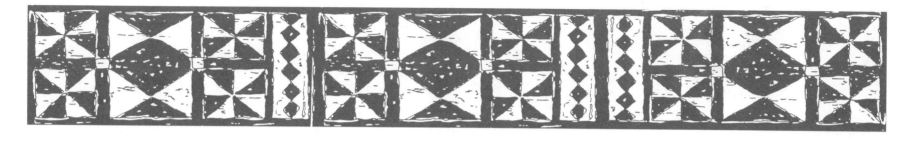

Storytelling and Folktales

"Storytelling is a way of encouraging children to read, to use their imagination and to explore their culture. It has an historical importance that allows storytellers to explain, in story form, about the Middle Passage and about families being separated during slavery. Storytelling allows future generations to learn where they came from."

DEBBIE KIRKLAND, STORYTELLER

Everyone likes a good story. Stories can make you laugh, teach an important lesson, or help pass on family and cultural information. African American folktales (or storytelling, as it is often called) date back to slavery. Storytelling was a way for African slaves to escape for a time to another world and to remember their homeland. So telling tales and singing songs became a big part of the slaves' culture.

At first, the tales were about things that happened in Africa. But as time went on, they also included the experiences of slaves in America. Often the tales were like a code through which the slaves could criticize or make fun of their masters. The tales often included animals such as bears, wolves, foxes, and turtles as the main characters. The most popular was a rabbit called Br'er or Bruh Rabbit, a character originally created in an old African folktale. These tales portrayed the rabbit, who was usually thought of as weak and not so smart, as a clever animal who outwitted the bigger and badder fox or bear. It is believed that slaves identified with the rabbit.

A Tall Tale

Even though African American folktales existed for many decades, it wasn't until the late nineteenth century that people began to collect and study them. Here is a tale that was frequently told by African American slaves. You'll also recognize elements of traditional European fairy tales.

The Wolf and Little Daughter

One day, Little Daughter was outside picking flowers. She lived in a cabin with her father that had a fence around it. Papa, as she called him, didn't want Little Daughter to run around in the forest where there were lots of wolves. He told her never to go out of the fence by herself. "I won't," she said.

One morning, when her father had to leave the house for a while, she decided she would go outside and look for flowers. While she was outside, she peeped through the fence. And just outside the fence was a beautiful yellow flower. It was so close to the fence that she decided it would be all right to go outside the fence and pick it.

When Little Daughter was outside the fence, she saw another pretty flower. She skipped over and picked that one, too. She saw another one and picked it. Then she picked another and another. They all smelled so sweet. She kept walking and picking, all the while singing a pretty song: "Tray-bla, tray-bla, cum qua, kimo." And as she was picking flowers to put in the vase for the kitchen table, she was getting farther away from the cabin.

Then, Little Daughter heard a noise. Standing in front of her was a great big wolf. The wolf said to her in a low, scary voice, "Sing that sweetest, goodest song again." So, Little Daughter sang it: "Tray-bla, tray-bla, cum qua, kimo."

Then, pit-pat-pit-pat, Little Daughter tiptoed toward the fence. Soon she heard big heavy steps coming behind her. It was the wolf! "Did you move?" he said in the same low voice.

"No, dear wolf. What occasion would I have to move?" said Little Daughter.

"Sing that sweetest, goodest song again," he said.

Little Daughter sang the song again: "Tray-bla, tray-bla, cum qua, kimo." The wolf was gone.

Little Daughter slowly tiptoed closer toward the fence. Once again, she heard loud footsteps coming behind her. She turned around and there stood the wolf. He said to her, "You moved."

Little Daughter said, "No, dear wolf. What occasion would I have to move?"

"Please sing that sweetest, goodest song again," said the big wolf.

Little Daughter sang the song again. The wolf was gone again.

This time, Little Daughter ran as fast as she could, pit-pat-pit-pat. She was close to the fence when she heard a loud pit-pat-pit-pat coming up behind her. Just then, Little Daughter slid inside the fence. Whack! She closed it fast—right in the big bad wolf's face. Now she was sweetest goodest safe.

In African American folktales such as "The Wolf and Little Daughter," the use of an animal and a child as the main characters dates back to the time when slaves told stories to their masters' children. Although the phrase "Tray-bla, tray-bla, cum qua, kimo" doesn't have a specific meaning, the individual words were remembered and used by slaves when telling this folktale.

Using your imagination, work together with your friends or classmates to create your own folktale.

Make Your Own Folktale

Here's What You Need

- [ ] 3 or more friends/classmates
- [ ] medium-size box
- [ ] pencils
- [ ] index cards
- [ ] timer

Here's What You Do

1 Sit in a circle around the box with your friends or classmates.

2 Have each player write down on an index card the type of animal he or she would like to include in the story. Put all the index cards in the box.

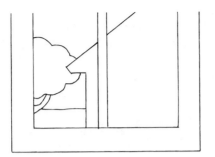

3 Shake the box around, then ask one player to choose a card. The animal written on that card will be one of the subjects of the story. Now empty the rest of the cards from the box.

4 Have everyone take another blank card and write on it the name of a person he or she would like to include in the story. Put the cards in the box.

5 Shake the box around and have a different player choose a card. The person written on that card will be another subject of the story. Empty the box.

6 Have everyone take another blank card, and this time write a location where the story should take place. It could be in the woods, on a beach, at a park, in school, in outer space, and so on. Put the cards in the box.

7 Shake the box around, then let another player pick a card. The place written on the card is the location of the story.

8 Now that you have some of the key elements of your tale, the storytelling can begin. Set the timer for 2 minutes. Using the elements on the index cards, the first player can begin to make up your story. When the timer buzzes, that player must stop telling the first part of the story. Reset the timer and have the next player continue the story where the last player left off. Each player should have a turn at making up the next part of the story until you all agree the story is complete!

9 Don't stop there. Shake the box and choose cards for other subjects and places and tell another story!

STORYTELLING TRADITION

African American folktales aren't just about animals and children. Some tales are ghost tales told as bedtime stories. In "The Peculiar Such Thing," the main character, a young fellow who lives alone in a one-room cabin, sees a strange-looking critter with a long tail one evening. While trying to kill it with his ax, he only chops off its tail. Every evening afterward, he hears the voice of the critter asking for its tail back.

Another popular folktale is "The People Could Fly," which tells of slaves who could magically fly away to freedom. The story is based on the belief that many Africans, before they became slaves, had the power to walk on air and fly away whenever they wanted. Once taken onto slave ships, they lost their wings and forgot how to fly. While laboring in the fields, some of the slaves' magical power returned. They would climb aboard a magical hoe and fly away. It is a tale that stirs the imagination and fosters the belief that almost anything is possible.

Hair Braiding

> "I took to wearing my hair in cornrows for most of the summer—a style that satisfied both my mother's desire for a 'natural' hairstyle and my grandmother's conception of acceptable hairstyling for an African American child."

NOLIWE M. ROOKS, PROFESSOR/AUTHOR

(FROM THE BOOK *HAIR RAISING: BEAUTY, CULTURE, AND AFRICAN AMERICAN WOMEN*, RUTGERS UNIVERSITY PRESS)

Dozens of various braided hairstyles are worn by African American women and men. The styles, which have unique names like cornrows, box braids, and French braids, all have their origin on the continent of Africa. Dating back to as long ago as 3000 B.C., young princesses in ancient Egypt sometimes wore what were called "braided locks of youth." The style was also used on wigs worn by men as a symbol of status. Made from human hair, palm leaf fibers, or wool, the wigs were braided or twisted, and covered with beeswax, which helped keep the braids in place. That process of twisting hair with beeswax is used today by people who wear their hair in **dreadlocks.**

Even though hair braiding in Africa was used as a way to look attractive, it was also used for several other reasons. Some regions used certain braided styles to mark special occasions while others used them to identify a person's age. In some cultures, the styles were very extravagant, with people using ornaments such as shells, flat bones, and beads to decorate their braids. Some styles were so detailed and complex that they could take from several hours to a whole day to finish. Hair braiding is a technique that takes a great deal of skill and patience.

Cornrowing (braiding hair close to the scalp) is one of the most popular and oldest hair-braiding techniques. It is believed the hairstyle got its name because it resembles the pattern of kernels on an ear of corn. Cornrows are also often braided in a straight rowed pattern that is similar to the rows of corn in a cornfield.

For many African Americans, cornrowing has more than just a cultural relevance. Throughout the 1970s, mothers cornrowed their daughters' hair as a matter of convenience. The style would last several days before it had to be rebraided.

Over the next few decades, cornrowing became more popular as braiders developed new and interesting styles. Today, cornrows have been made even more popular by rap artists and athletes. For a firsthand try at how they're done, braid a friend's hair using this simplified version of creating cornrows.

Cornrows

Here's What You Need

- [ ] 2 participants, each with hair at least 5 inches (13 cm) long
- [ ] comb
- [ ] hair bands
- [ ] small rubber bands
- [ ] hair clips
- [ ] scarf (optional)

Here's What You Do

1 Before starting, comb the hair through thoroughly to loosen the curl. Starting from the front of the hairline, part the hair down the center to the nape of the neck. Gather one side of the parted hair into a hair clip or band.

2 Using the comb, part the other half of the hair into two equal sections. This part should also be made from the hairline to the neck. Secure each section with a hair band.

strand. Each time you bring the right or left strand under the center strand, it will become the new center strand.

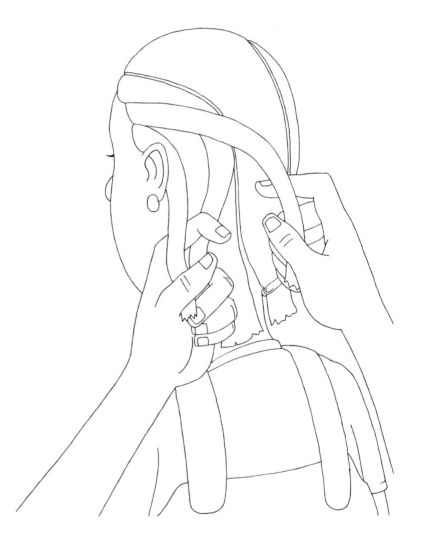

3 Start with the section closest to the ear. Starting at the hairline, divide the hair into three equal strands. Begin to weave the strands into a cornrow: a threefold braid that will lie flat on the head. First bring the right strand under the center strand as shown. The right strand is now the center strand. Then bring the left strand under the center

4 Pick up ½ inch (1.25 cm) of hair on the right side (from the scalp), then pair it with the right strand and hold it. Pick up a ½ inch (1.25 cm) of hair on the left side and pair it with the left strand. Bring the left strand under the center strand.

5 To complete the first section, continue to pick up pieces of hair from the scalp (following the process in step 4) and weave the strands into the cornrow. Be sure to cornrow the section to the end of the hair. If the hair is fine, secure the end with a rubber band to keep the ends in place.

6 Repeat the same process on the other section on that side of the head. When you're done, part the hair on the other side into two sections and cornrow them also, following steps 3 to 5. If your friend would like to maintain the cornrow style overnight or for several days, tell her to wrap her head with a silk scarf before going to sleep.

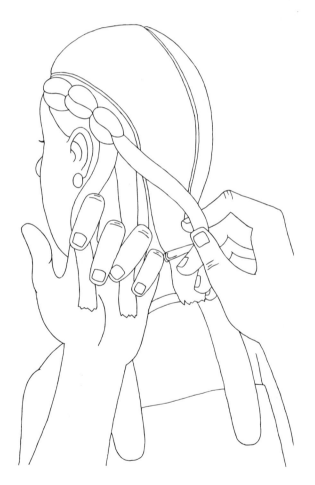

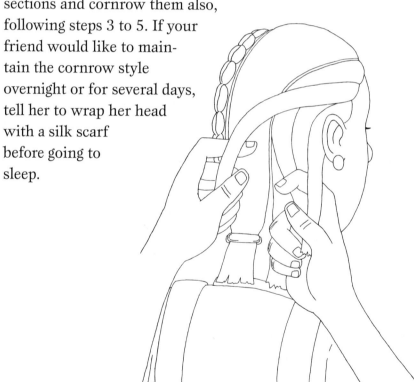

Suku Kolese Koroba

HAIR-BRAIDING TRADITION

The Yoruba people of Africa have specific names for cornrow styles, such as Kolese (without legs), Koroba (bucket), and Suku (basket).

Quilting

> *During slavery, women used whatever scraps of cloth they could get to make quilts. They made them from old dresses or patches they got from their masters' wives. Some of those cloths were left over from the tailors who made their husbands' clothes. But the main reason slaves began making quilts was so that their families wouldn't freeze during the winter months.*
>
> THELMA MATTOX, QUILTER

Quilts are beautiful, but many represent more than just something that is used to cover the bed or to keep warm. The craft of **quilting** (making quilts) is popular in many cultures and has a history that dates back hundreds of years. African American **patchwork** (using small pieces of cloth to make a pattern) quilt making is believed to have started with slaves who were influenced by woven textiles made in Central and West Africa. Over time, their descendants made quilting a tradition that has been passed on from generation to generation.

Slaves who lived in cold cabins made quilts out of whatever scrap fabric they could find. In later years, quilt makers made the quilts warmer by adding cotton interlining and **muslin** (a woven cotton fabric) backing. Most African American quilts feature geometric patterns with unique names such as "Rising Sun," "Wedding Ring," "Sawtooth," and "Pineapple."

Many African American women in the South continue to hold weekly or monthly quilting bees, where they help each

QUILTS WITH A MESSAGE

Storytelling isn't limited to the spoken word. Early quilters often found a way to relate their life experiences and beliefs onto their quilts. The Smithsonian's National Museum of American History in Washington, D.C., recently displayed several quilts made during the nineteenth century. One of the quilts, "The Bible Quilt," told of several incidents that took place in the Old and New Testaments. It was made in 1886 by Harriet Powers, an African American farm woman who lived in Georgia. Powers's quilt contains appliquéd images of the Garden of Eden, Cain and Abel, and the Last Supper. First displayed at a cotton fair in Athens, Georgia, the quilt was later bought from Ms. Powers by a young artist named Jennie Smith. Present-day New Jersey quilter Thelma Mattox continues that tradition by making quilts that tell stories. One of her quilts contains embroidered images of every U.S. president and another features all the state birds.

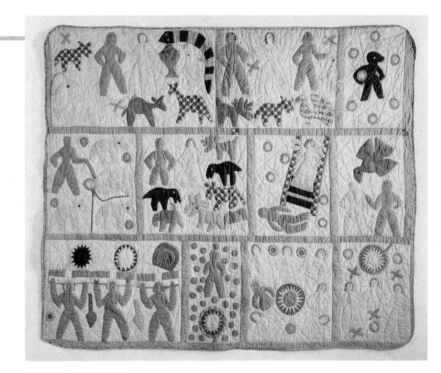

The Bible Quilt, 1886.

other sew quilts. Depending on the dedication of the quilter, an entire quilt can be made in a few weeks or months. Some quilts that include **embroidery** (decorations created with a needle and thread) or are made using many different pieces of fabric can take as long as a year to make.

The quilt pattern you're about to make is a simple one called "Triangles." It can be done alone or with a group of people. Thelma Mattox, who has been quilting for many years, first learned to sew at the age of seven while growing up in South Carolina. This quilting style is one of her favorites. Since some portions of it require using a sewing machine, you may need the help of a parent or teacher.

Miniature Quilt

Here's What You Need

- scissors
- ½ yard (45 cm) of fabric in each of two colors
- sewing machine (requires adult help)
- bag of cotton balls or Poly-Fil (polyester fiber)
- needle
- 2 spools of thread, one to match each color of fabric
- white lace

Here's What You Do

1 Cut twelve 6-by-6-inch (15-by-15-cm) squares out of each piece of fabric.

2 Fold each square into a triangular shape.

3 With an adult's help or supervision, use the sewing machine to sew closed one short side of a triangle up to the corner. Then sew the long side and the other short side, leaving a $2^{1}/_{2}$-inch (6-cm) opening at the corner as shown. Do this to all of the triangles.

4 Turn each triangle inside out so that the stitching doesn't show. Stuff each triangle with cotton balls or Poly-Fil. The amount of stuffing you use determines how thick or heavy your quilt will be.

5 When all the triangles have been stuffed, fold the openings inward and use a needle and thread to hand-sew them closed.

6 To make the first "square" of your quilt, take four triangles (two of each color) and lay them flat. Face the pointed ends of the triangles toward the center. Use triangles of one color on the top and bottom, and triangles of the other color on the left and right. This is the pattern for each square of your quilt.

7 Folding each inner corner down slightly, sew the sides of the triangles together. For this step, you can use either the sewing machine or a needle and thread.

8 Using the remaining triangles, repeat steps 6 and 7 to make five more squares.

9 Hand-sew pairs of squares together so that you have three pairs. Then sew all the pairs together in three rows with two pairs in each row.

10 Measure and cut two strips of lace that are 13 inches (33 cm) in length and 1 inch (2.5 cm) wide and two strips that are 19 inches (48 cm) long and 1 inch (2.5 cm) wide. With an adult's help or supervision, use the

sewing machine to sew the strips of lace to each edge of your miniature quilt, making seams at each corner. Now that your quilt is done, you can give it away as a holiday gift or use it to decorate your doll's bed.

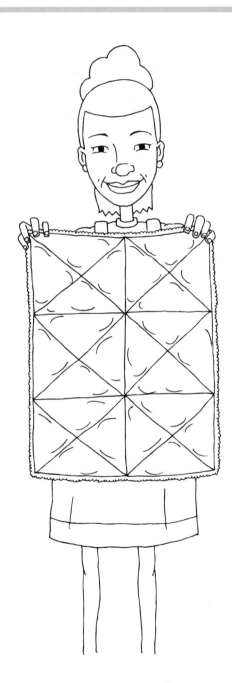

QUILTING TRADITION

Some quilts are made with a technique called **appliqué,** which involves stitching patterns of cutout fabric on a solid background. This is said to have come from a tradition of royal tapestries made in Benin, a republic of West Africa. Many slaves were taken from that region and brought to Georgia.

III
CRAFTS

Craft making is fun and gives you the opportunity to be creative. The crafts in this section also will allow you to re-create colorful and expressive objects used by Africans and African Americans in ceremonies, rituals, and everyday life.

A big part of African culture is utilizing the available resources from nature for daily living and to create things for pleasure. The crafts you will make in this section were originally made centuries ago from items such as fruit, wood, metals, animal skins, dyes, and clays.

Before there were buckets or pails, something had to be used to carry water from the wells back to the villages. After its soft middle was scooped out, the calabash, a large tropical fruit, was used for carrying water. Clothing, masks, and drums were, and continue to be, a big part of African

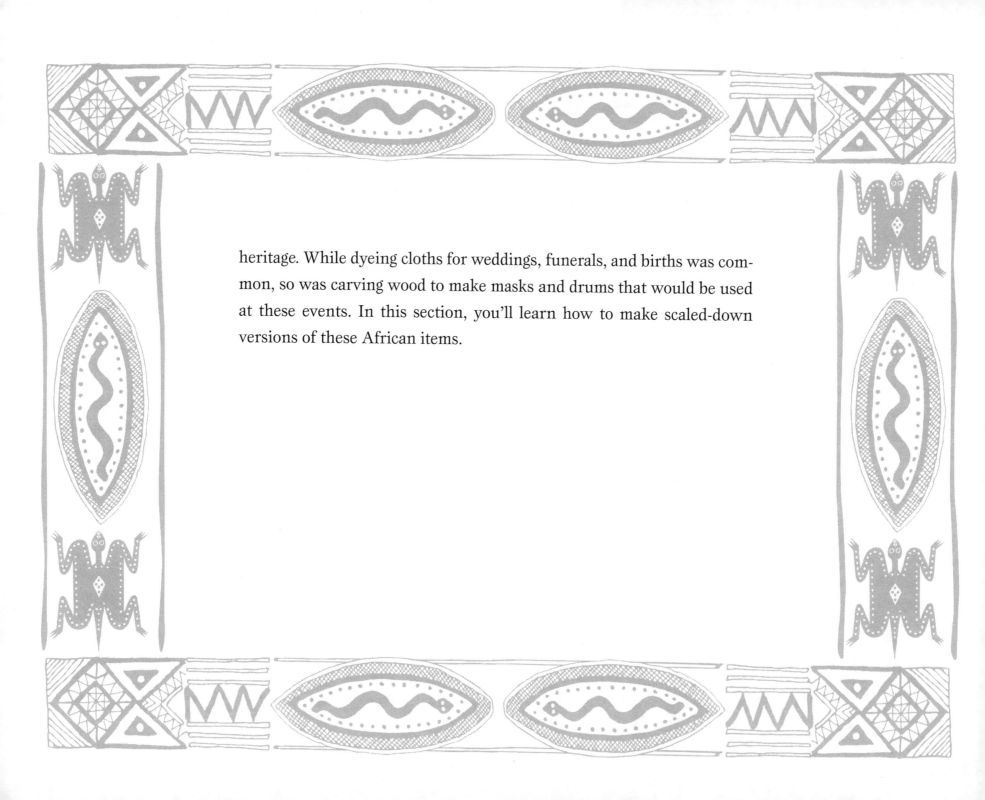

heritage. While dyeing cloths for weddings, funerals, and births was common, so was carving wood to make masks and drums that would be used at these events. In this section, you'll learn how to make scaled-down versions of these African items.

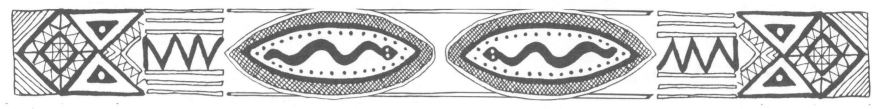

Calabash

A **calabash** is a hard-shelled fruit that grows in the tropics. In Nigeria, calabashes were used to hold and carry water and as decorations. Like watermelons and pumpkins, calabashes grow on vines. Villagers would carve a hole into the top and remove the fruit inside. Then they would dry the calabash shells by either baking them or leaving them out under the hot rays of the sun. The shells were then decorated with beautiful patterns created with clays and dyes.

Because of their unique shapes, other versions of the calabash, known as calabash gourds, were often used to make water bottles, spoons, pipes, and musical instruments. The gourds, which grow in varying sizes and shapes, were given interesting names, such as dipper, club, kettle, trough, and dolphin. The round calabash, though, is the most widely used among the people of Nigeria and surrounding villages. The calabash only grows in tropical climates, but here is an interesting way to make a model of a calabash.

43

Decorative Calabash

Here's What You Need

- 2 large balloons
- ¹/₂ cup (120 mL) flour
- bowl
- 1 cup (240 mL) warm water
- small stick
- newspaper
- needle
- sandpaper
- paints

Here's What You Do

1 Blow up the balloons and tie them tightly.

2 Pour all the flour and water into the bowl. Mix the ingredients with the stick to create a thick paste.

3 Using enough newspaper to cover both balloons, tear the newspaper into narrow strips. Dip the strips into the bowl, allowing the excess mixture to drip off the strips.

4 Cover the balloons with two layers of paste-covered newspaper. Allow the newspaper to dry for 3 or 4 hours.

5 When you are sure the newspaper is dry, pop the balloons with the needle. Lightly sand the bottom of your calabash to make it flat.

6 Decorate your calabash with bright colored paints, then use it to decorate your room!

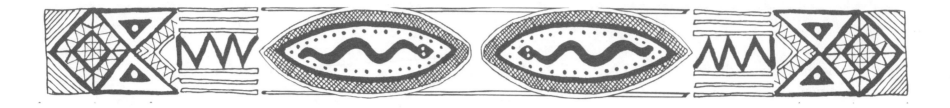

Adire (Tie-Dyeing)

You've probably seen a tie-dyed T-shirt, if you don't actually have one. What you may not know is that tie-dyed clothing and cloths were commonly made by people living in West and East Africa. In Tanzania and Kenya, tie-dyed cloths were being made as early as 1817. At that time, tie-dyed patterns were used to show a person's high ranking in society. They were also worn at weddings and funerals.

Adire was the name given to fabrics dyed by the Yoruba people of Nigeria. The dyer would stencil or hand-draw design patterns onto the cloth using cassaba starch, a product that comes from the cassaba flower. When the fabric was dyed, the dye would cover every area except where the starch was used.

In the United States, thousands of African American children learn to make African tie-dyed fabrics at cultural fairs and parties. Before making your own tie-dye creation, be sure to dress in old, comfortable clothing. Things could get a little messy.

Tie-Dyed T-Shirt

Here's What You Need

- large white T-shirt
- scissors
- thick string
- long stick or broom-stick
- several cold-water dyes of different colors (available at any art supply store)
- 2 buckets
- water

Here's What You Do

1 Tie three knots in the T-shirt—one at the top, another near the center, and one at the bottom. Cut three 10-inch (25-cm) pieces of string.

2 Wrap the T-shirt around the stick, leaving a little room at one end to hold the stick while dipping. Using one piece

of string to tie the top of the T-shirt to the stick, wrap the string (twice) around the top knot, then tie it. Wrap the remaining pieces of string around the other knots, tying them as well.

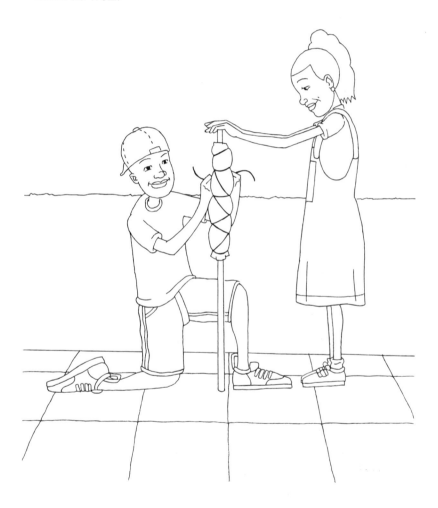

3 Following the package instructions on the package of dye, mix the dye with water in one of the buckets. Now dip the stick into the bucket so that the T-shirt is completely submerged. Leave the stick in the bucket for several minutes.

4 While the stick is still in the first bucket, fill the second bucket with plain water.

5 Lift the stick out of the dye bucket and let the excess dye drain from the T-shirt into the bucket.

6 Cut the string from the T-shirt and rinse the T-shirt in the bucket of plain water.

7 Hang the T-shirt outdoors on a clothesline or over the branch of a tree. Let it dry for several hours.

8 When the T-shirt has dried, tie new knots in it and repeat steps 2 to 7 using three new pieces of string and a different color dye. Repeat the process several times. When you're done, you'll have a beautiful creation to give to a friend or wear to school.

TIE-DYE TRADITION

Indigo dye, a blue dye made from the indigo plant, is often used by Nigerian people because the color blue helps reduce the glare of sunlight in their hot sunny climate.

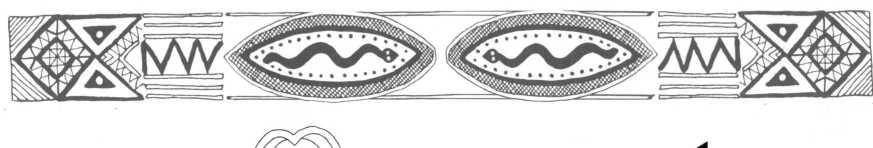

Mask Making

Tribal masks come in many different sizes and colors. They were used by Africans in religious ceremonies, celebrations, wars, and dances in honor of ancestors. These masks were, and still are, worn by people in Nigeria, Liberia, and other regions of Africa. Some masks were made to cover the face. Others were worn over the entire head.

Because it was easier to cut, mask carvers often used wood from young trees to make masks. Strips of animal skin, rough leaves, or pieces of bone were rubbed over the surface of the finished masks to make them smooth. Many masks were darkened by dipping them in mud or by slightly burning them. Some carvers gave their masks a final shine by rubbing them with vegetable oils. Although most masks were carved from wood, some also contained brass, metal, mirrors, and copper.

Long and square or short and round, the faces of African masks are as varied as the faces of people. Masks that were made for battle might have large, scary features such as big teeth and large eyes; but masks worn in religious ceremonies were decorated with colorful headpieces made with earrings, vegetable fibers, pieces of cloth, cowrie shells, or beads. In America today, African masks are sold to hang on the wall as decorative artworks. Museums around the world exhibit masks from all provinces of Africa.

Here's a chance to make your own original tribal mask. Make it silly or scary, beautiful or ugly. It's guaranteed that no one will have a mask that looks like yours.

Tribal Mask

Here's What You Need

- newspaper
- 6-by-6-inch (15-by-15-cm) piece of Styrofoam
- scissors
- pencil
- paper plate
- glue
- instant papier-mâché mix (available at craft stores)
- water
- paste
- large bowl
- paintbrush
- water-based paints
- brown yarn
- thick thread or string
- large colored beads
- 2 long shoe strings (optional)

Here's What You Do

1 Lay several sheets of newspaper over your work space.

2 From the Styrofoam, cut out two small pieces to be the nose and mouth of your mask. Make them any shape you like.

3 Using a pencil, draw two eyes on the paper plate. Cut out the eyeholes.

4 Attach the Styrofoam nose and mouth to the paper plate with glue. Allow the glue to dry.

5 Use the pencil to poke a small hole in each side of the plate. The holes will be for the string to go through so that you can wear or hang the mask.

6 Make the papier-mâché by mixing paper, water, and paste in a large bowl according to the package instructions. Cover both sides of the plate with papier-mâché. Be sure not to cover the eyes or the holes in the side of the mask. Bend the sides of the plate back slightly before the papier-mâché dries so that the plate easily frames your face.

7 Allow the mask to dry for several hours. After it has dried, use the paints to decorate the mask however you like. Let the paint dry.

8 For the hair, cut three pieces of brown yarn that are each 12 inches (30 cm) long. Glue them along the top edge of the mask so that they fall down past the holes on the side of the mask.

9 Make earrings for the mask by threading each of two pieces of string about 7 inches (18 cm) in length with seven or eight beads. Poke two additional small holes, one on each side of the mask. Then thread the earrings through and tie them onto the mask.

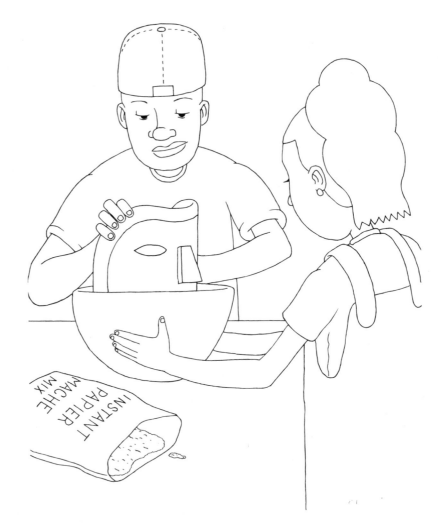

10 Now thread the shoe strings (or regular string) through the original two holes of the mask. Tie the strings together so that you can either wear the mask or hang it in your room.

MASK-MAKING TRADITION

In small villages along the Niger River, the Marka and Bamabara people use mythological masks in ceremonies they hold at night. Dancers, dressed in costumes made from wild rice straw, perform dances to symbolize the creation of the world. They are followed by people carrying masks and wearing costumes. The main mask is painted with stars and grains of corn, and is in the image of an animal with horns. The horns are a symbol of beauty. Fringes of cloth and leather on the mask represent cultivated fields and flowing water. Other symbolic masks, including three lion masks that represent power, strength, and the dignity of kings, pass through the ceremony in order of importance.

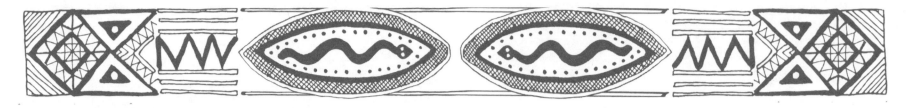

Drums

Boom, boom, boom, pop! pop! Boom, boom, boom, pop! pop! pop! goes the drum. To most ears, the beating of a drum means dancing, marching, or just keeping rhythm. But in Africa, the beats, rhythms, and sounds created on the drum were also used as a form of communication. The way a drum was played could show joy, pain, or anger. It could also tell of the birth of a child, initiation into adulthood, or a wedding, or it could be a call for help or a warning.

The drum could easily be called the most important instrument in Central Africa. In addition to making music for celebrations, drums helped people in remote places send messages. The talking drum, played in many parts of Africa, could even imitate the sound of a human voice.

In Ghana and many other African villages, drum making was a unifying activity that brought men of the villages together. Using wood from trees and animal skins, fathers and sons made drums that were to be played during ceremonies. Drum-making tradition began as early as the seventh century, and various techniques continued to be developed well into the fifteenth century.

DRUMS

Congo music, an African version of Cuban rumba music, is where the popular conga drum gets its name. Created in Congo, a country in Central Africa formerly known as Zaire, Congo music often features Congolese kettledrums, which are very similar in shape to **conga drums** used in Latin and African American dance music. While **kettledrums** are played with sticks and supported by wooden frames, the African American and Latin conga drum sits on the ground and is played by hand. Other African drums that are similar in shape and sound to the kettledrum are the **badima**, a pedestal-based drum used in funerals, and the **mankuntu,** cylindrical drums that have various pitches. (Cylindrical means shaped like or made of a hollow body, with straight sides and a flat round top and bottom.) Both are played by the Tonga people of Zambia. Other popular Tonga drums are the **musimbo** and the **masabe.**

The Nigerian *dun-dun* drum is called a talking drum because the sound it makes is close to the Yoruba language. Although the version of the talking drum you're about to make isn't as sturdy or durable as an original one, from it you can get an understanding of the drum sounds enjoyed by the people of Africa.

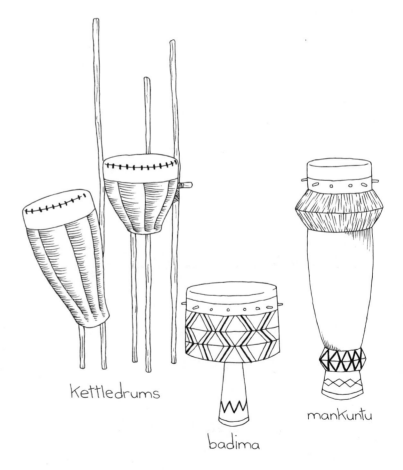

Kettledrums

badima

mankuntu

Talking Drum

Here's What You Need

- cement or strong glue
- 2 plastic 8-inch (20-cm) –diameter flowerpots
- scissors
- 1 yard (.91 m) of flat rubber inner tubing (can be purchased at a rubber company)
- ruler
- screwdriver (requires adult help)
- 2 yards (1.8 m) of rawhide lacing (available at fabric stores or leather manufacturers)
- water
- cloth
- adult helper

Here's What You Do

1 Glue or cement the pots together at the bottoms so that the drain holes match up. Allow the glue to dry.

2 Cut two pieces of rubber tubing that are 1 inch (2.5 cm) larger than the openings of the flowerpots. With adults' help, use a screwdriver to poke eight holes around the edges of the rubber that are 2 inches (5 cm) apart and ½ inch (1 cm) from the edge.

3 Soak the rubber and the rawhide lacing for 45 minutes in lukewarm water to soften them before using. Pat the rubber and the lacing dry with a cloth.

4 Lay one piece of rubber flat on a table, then place the opening of one of the pots over it. Place the other piece on top of the opening of the other pot. Thread the lacing

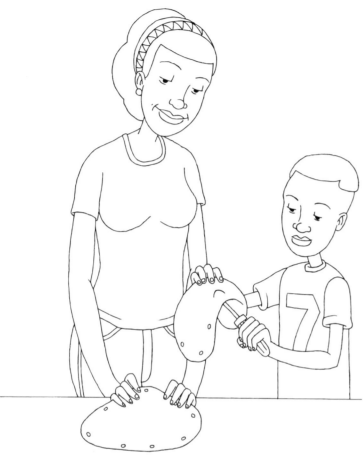

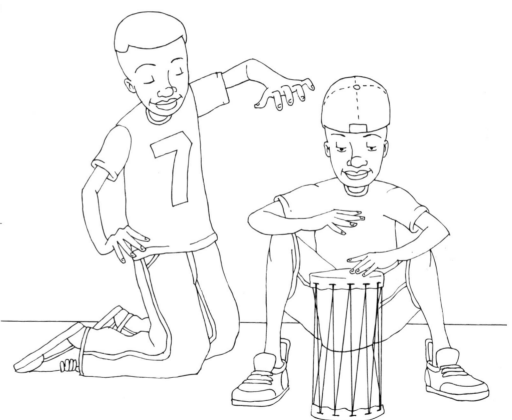

through the holes in the rubber from the top of the drum to the bottom as shown. Be sure that the lacing is tight enough so that both pieces of rubber are stretched taut. This will ensure that your drum will produce the right sounds.

5 Allow the drum to dry for 10 to 12 hours before using.

IV GAMES

Sure, games are played for fun. But some African games, such as *kei* (also known as *seega*), were also used to teach strategy. Originally played in Egypt and Sierra Leone, this game (which is similar to checkers) can be played with as many as 40 pieces on a board of 100 squares. African kings and members of their royal courts enjoyed playing board games. The Ashanti kings in Ghana often played on boards made of solid gold.

Kings weren't the only ones who played games. Children and adults living in small African villages drew games they could play on the dirt or sand. They used pebbles, sticks, and leaves as game pieces. Most African games, such as *muraburaba,* created in Lesotho, and *yote,* which came from West

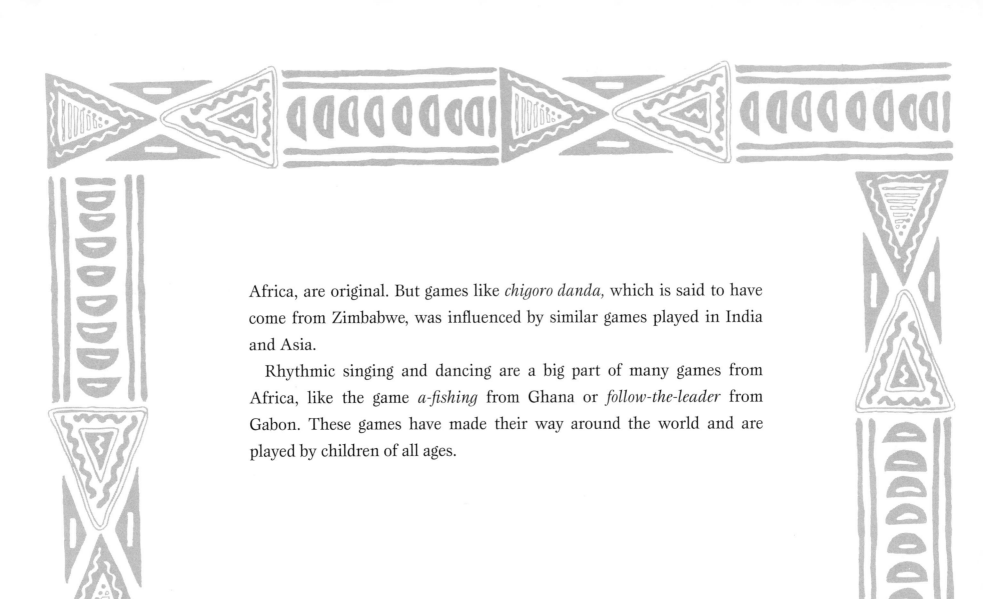

Africa, are original. But games like *chigoro danda,* which is said to have come from Zimbabwe, was influenced by similar games played in India and Asia.

Rhythmic singing and dancing are a big part of many games from Africa, like the game *a-fishing* from Ghana or *follow-the-leader* from Gabon. These games have made their way around the world and are played by children of all ages.

Mancala

Mancala is a popular game that is played in many parts of Africa. Although it's hard to determine exactly where it originated, one story tells of a ruler of the Bushongo tribe in Congo, who brought the game back after a visit to Egypt. One sure thing is that mancala dates back thousands of years. Game boards carved in stone were discovered in the Egyptian temples of Karnak and Luxor.

Although mancala is basically played the same way everywhere, it goes by several different names. People in some African regions call it *awari* or *wari*. West Africans call the game *owari*. Mancala boards can be purchased in many stores, but half the fun is creating one of your own, as in this activity.

Mancala

Here's What You Need

- scissors
- egg carton
- 1-cup (240-mL) measuring cup
- flour
- large bowl
- glue
- cold water
- large spoon
- newspaper
- paintbrush
- paints
- piece of thick cardboard, wood, or Styrofoam that is slightly longer and wider than the egg carton
- 2 small paper cups
- 48 beads or marbles
- 2 players

Here's How You Make the Board

1 Cut off the top of an empty egg carton.

2 Prepare a papier-mâché mixture by pouring 1 cup (249 mL) of flour into the bowl. Add a few drops of glue. Fill the measuring cup with water, then slowly pour the water into the bowl, stirring the mixture until there are no lumps. The papier-mâché mixture should be sticky, so use your judgment when adding water. You may not need to use the entire cup.

3 Tear off several narrow strips of newspaper, then dip them into the mixture. Cover the egg carton with the papier-mâché. Let the papier-mâché dry for several hours, then paint the carton with your own design.

4 After the paint dries, glue the bottom of the carton onto the piece of cardboard, wood, or Styrofoam. This will be the base of the mancala board. At each end of the carton, glue one small paper cup onto the base. These cups are called "mancalas." Each player "owns" the mancala to his or her left.

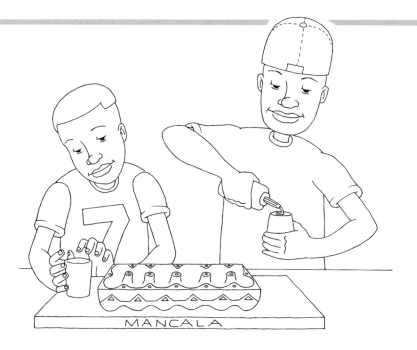

Here's How You Play

1 Each player sits at one long side of the mancala board. The six holes in front of each player are his or her holes. To start the game, player 1 places four marbles in each hole on the board.

2 Player 2, starting from the hole on the far right (on his or her side of the board), picks up all the marbles in that hole. Continuing counterclockwise, that player drops one marble in each hole until all the marbles from his or her hand have been dropped. If the player comes to his or her mancala and has one marble left, the player may place it in the mancala. If the player has more than one marble left, he or she must pass the mancala and place the marbles in the next few holes. Players cannot drop marbles into their opponent's mancala. Simply skip the mancala and drop the marble in the next hole.

3 Next, player 1 picks up all the marbles in the farthest hole on his or her right and drops them in the holes, moving counterclockwise, and following the same procedure as the previous player. As the game continues, if the right-hand hole is empty when it's time for a new turn, that player should pick up marbles from the next hole on the right.

4 Players continue until there are no marbles left in any of the holes. The player with the most marbles in his or her mancala wins.

Little Sally Walker

The musical game Little Sally Walker has been played by African American children in the North and the South for decades. A fun game that involves singing and dancing, it is derived from African games like "What Is Big?" from Zimbabwe, which also uses movement and chanting. The title of the song used in the game is "Shake It to the One That You Love the Best." A game that requires lots of room, Little Sally Walker is best played outdoors. Have fun!

Little Sally Walker

Here's What You Need

☐ at least 5 players

Here's How You Play

1 Players form a circle around one person. The person in the center is "Sally." While moving around in a circle, the other players hold hands and sing the song. See lyrics.

2 While the song is sung, Sally dances around and acts out the words of the song. When the phrase "Shake it to the east, shake it to the west, shake it to the one that you love the best" is sung, Sally moves back and forth toward the players, acting as if she's about to choose her replacement.

3 When the song comes to an end, Sally picks a player to take her place inside the circle. The game is over when everyone has had a chance to be Sally.

(There are no specific movements to this game. Each player who has a turn as Sally can act out the song with whatever dance movements he or she wishes. Moving your body to the left and then to the right is the only suggested movement for the phrase "Shake it to the east, shake it to the west.")

SALLY'S SONG: SHAKE IT TO THE ONE THAT YOU LOVE THE BEST

Little Sally Walker, sitting in a saucer,
ride, Sally, ride.
Wipe your weeping eyes,
put your hand on your hip, and let your backbone slip.
Shake it to the east, shake it to the west,
shake it to the one that you love the best.
Ride, Sally, ride.

Little Sally Walker, sitting in a saucer,
crying for the old man to come for the dollar,
ride, Sally, ride.
Put your hand on your hip, and let your backbone slip.
Shake it to the east, shake it to the west,
shake it to the one that you love the best.
Ride, Sally, ride.

Muraburaba

Lesotho is one of the smallest countries in Africa. You can easily find it on the map because it is surrounded by South Africa, another African country. It is believed that **muraburaba** was invented by Lesotho shepherds herding their flocks on the hillsides. Herding was pretty dull work, so the shepherds played the game to help the time pass more quickly.

The great thing about *muraburaba* is that it can be played on a large piece of paper or cardboard, as in this activity, or in the sand or dirt.

Muraburaba

Here's How You Make the Board

1 About 2 inches (5 cm) from the edge of the cardboard, draw a large square. Then draw another square inside the square that is about 4 inches (10 cm) from the first square. Next, draw another square inside that one that is about 4 inches (10 cm) from the second square. The innermost square should be 3 inches (7½ cm) long and 3 inches (7½ cm) wide.

2 Draw two diagonal lines through the middle of the squares so that the corners of the squares are connected. Extend the lines just past the outer corner of the largest square.

3 Draw a horizontal line and a vertical line through the middle of the squares. All of your lines should meet in the center.

sure that one opponent uses one color of beads and the other opponent uses the other color. If you are using money, one opponent should use pennies and the other should use dimes.)

2 Taking turns, each player or team places a game piece on an empty circle. The goal is to be the first player or team to lay down three game pieces in a row. The pieces should be placed one after the other, either vertically, horizontally, or diagonally. When this happens, it is called a "strike." A player or team that makes a strike can remove one of the other opponent's game pieces from the board. As in tic-tac-toe, each team should think about blocking their opponent to keep them from making a strike.

3 Players continue putting all the pieces on the board in an effort to make strikes. When all the pieces are down, take turns moving them one space at a time to try and make more strikes. Players cannot jump over other game pieces. Pieces can only be moved from one circle to an adjoining open circle.

4 A player or team wins when the opponent has only two game pieces left and can't make another strike, or when the opponent is "trapped" or "blocked" and can't move any more game pieces.

4 Draw small circles wherever two or more lines intersect. When you're done, you should have a total of 25 circles.

Here's How You Play

1 The players sit on opposite sides of the board. Each player or team has 12 game pieces. (If you are using beads, make

Chigoro Danda

Chigoro Danda, a game also known as thumping sticks, was played by children in Zimbabwe. Because the word *danda* means "long stick" in an Indian language, many believe the game may have been brought to Africa by settlers from India. The children there call the game *Guli Danda*. African children have made the game their own by adding clapping and an African chant.

The exciting thing about playing games is that you can alter them any way you'd like. After you've played once, try coming up with a chant of your own . . . in English!

Chigoro Danda

- 3 sticks or poles that are each about 5 feet (152 cm) long and 3 inches (8 cm) thick

- 3 to 12 players (Only three players at a time can actually play the game. The other players sit or stand in a circle around the bars, and clap and sing until it is their turn.)

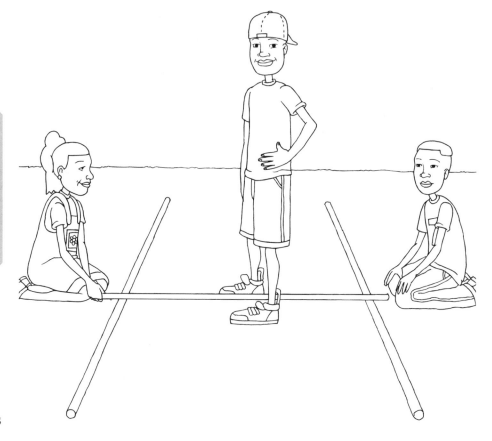

Here's What You Do

1 Lay two of the sticks on the ground parallel to each other and about 4 feet (122 cm) apart. Lay the third stick across the center of the parallel sticks.

2 Two players sit beside the crossbar (stick), one at each end. The third player stands between the parallel bars, straddling the crossbar.

3 The two players who are sitting lift the ends of the crossbar at the same time. Starting slowly, in a rhythmic motion, they tap the crossbar against the parallel bars.

4 The player in the center hops and steps lightly onto the crossbar in rhythm every time it hits the parallel bars, then hops off.

5 The other players awaiting their turn clap and sing *"Aiye chigoro danda chigoro."* (The word *chigoro* means "sound.")

6 The two players holding the crossbar increase the speed of their tapping, and the singers increase the speed of their clapping and singing. The player jumping must continue to hop and step onto the crossbar as it moves faster and faster. If the player fails to hop on the bar, he or she drops out of the game and one of the other players takes his or her place.

7 Players rotate so that everyone has an opportunity both to be the jumper and to hold the crossbar.

8 The player who can keep hopping onto the crossbar for the longest time is the winner.

V

CULTURE

Culture includes all the things that make a particular group of people unique—the way they dance; the sound of their music; and the words, phrases, and subjects used in their literature. Dance, music, and literature are special art forms that people of all cultures use to express themselves and their life history in the way they feel most comfortable. In this section, you'll get to know about gospel, jazz, and blues music; tap, contemporary, and ballet dancing; African American literature; and much more. And as you learn about each of these African American expressions, you'll have the opportunity to be a little creative, too!

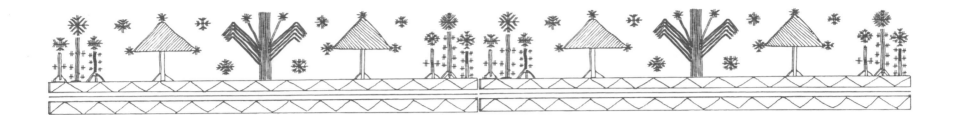

Music

Every form of African American music we listen to today—gospel, jazz, blues, rap, and soul (also known as rhythm and blues)—is an extension of traditional African music. In the days of slavery, the music the slaves brought from Africa was developed into new forms. Slaves didn't have the kind of drums or other instruments that were part of their culture, so they found other ways to create sound. Foot stomping, hand clapping, field hollers and call-and-response singing (traditions also popular in Africa) were the first methods they used. After slavery, African American music continued to be heard everywhere, from **jook joints** (small shack-like clubs where musicians played live music and people danced) to churches.

As early as the seventeenth century, free African Americans and slaves would perform African-sounding music at festivals held in Virginia, North Carolina, and New Orleans, Louisiana. Over the next few centuries, the lyrics of the music became influenced by African Americans' experiences in America. Blues songs, which were often sung loudly and with emotion like slave work songs, gave musicians the opportunity to sing about (sometimes in humorous ways) the problems in their lives. In this chapter, you will learn how the blues and other forms of African American music—gospel, jazz, soul, and rap—are extensions of one another. Each relies heavily on the tradition of call-and-response singing; each relays life experiences and expresses the African tradition of storytelling.

Blues, Gospel, and Soul

Let's say you're overjoyed that your report card this semester is brimming with good grades; Or maybe you're disappointed because you didn't get the kind of sneakers you wanted for your birthday. These things cause you to feel emotions you might want to share with a family member or friend. Three ways African Americans have developed to express an experience or feeling is through blues, gospel, and soul music. Even though each of these musical forms has influenced the others and they share some of the same characteristics, each has its own unique sound and history.

BLUES

The Mississippi Delta region of Louisiana is the birthplace of the blues. As early as the late 1890s, blues singers were creating songs about the problems in their lives, such as low wages and lost loves. Accompanied by a guitar or some other simple instrument, singers performed their songs at outdoor gatherings and in jook joints. Most of the blues songs created during that time were played at a slow or mid-tempo pace. The guitar (and in later years, piano) chords and bass lines were usually played in the lower register of the scales. This sound further emphasized the "bluesy" feeling of the lyrics, which were frequently repeated throughout the song.

The origin of the blues dates back to the days of slavery, but the earliest formal recognition came in the early 1900s. This was when Ma Rainey, the Mother of the Blues, began performing, and W. C. Handy recorded the songs "The Memphis Blues" and "St. Louis Blues." By the 1920s, the popularity of the blues had spread throughout the United States.

Some of the earliest famous blues singers, such as Bessie Smith and Alberta Hunter, were known for singing vaudeville blues, a style that was popular among both blacks and whites. Because these songs were performed as part of traveling stage shows, they were altered to appeal to all audiences. The music was played by small bands who slightly changed the format of the blues. Instead of being played with a blues sound all the way through, the songs were given a more traditional-sounding introduction.

In the late 1920s, however, down-home blues replaced vaudeville blues. Record company representatives began traveling to the South to record local blues singers, who accompanied themselves with just a guitar or piano. This was the original sound of the blues. The music was so loved that major record labels decided to bring African American artists North to record **race records** (songs recorded by African American musicians). Many of the original race records, such as "Hound Dog" and "Jailhouse Rock," were re-recorded by white singers such as Elvis Presley. Popular African American blues artists who emerged over the next century included B. B. King, Muddy Waters, and John Lee Hooker.

GOSPEL

Gospel music is a way of expressing spirituality through song. Gospel was influenced by a form of singing brought from Africa by slaves called call and response. In call-and-response singing, after one person sang a line, the rest of the group would repeat the same, or possibly a different, line. This practice became a big part of gospel music. As African Americans began establishing their own churches, they adapted this musical and oral tradition to their praise of God. Washboards, triangles, and tambourines were the first instruments used to accompany the singing. Eventually, cymbals, drums, pianos, and guitars were sometimes used as well.

Gospel music includes spirituals and hymns, which are slower paced and often sung by soloists and choirs. **Jubilee** (a

Southern form of gospel music that is rhythmically similar to the blues) is usually sung by quartets. One of the most famous gospel songs, "Precious Lord, Take My Hand," was written in 1932 by a Philadelphia minister, Charles A. Tindley.

The list of singers who have had their impact on gospel is endless. Mahalia Jackson, the Dixie Hummingbirds, and Shirley Caesar are just a few. Gospel also played a major role during the Civil Rights movement, providing freedom songs, such as "We Shall Overcome," that helped to inspire a people trying to gain equality. Gospel also set the stage for another form of music that got its start in the 1960s—soul.

SOUL

A perfect example of someone who made the transition from gospel to soul music is Aretha Franklin. A vocalist who started singing in her father's church, she used her voice trained in gospel and church-influenced piano playing to make popular soul records beginning in the 1960s. Soul music was originally called rhythm and blues. The name, which was developed to describe dance and blues music made by African Americans, was coined in 1949 by Billboard, a popular-music magazine.

By the 1960s, the Civil Rights movement had developed and the word soul was used to describe several things in African American culture, including food and music. The word reflected the pride African Americans were beginning to feel during that period of time.

Franklin, eventually dubbed the "Queen of Soul," and James Brown, the "Godfather of Soul," took the call-and-response and free-style elements of gospel and included them in songs that perfectly expressed the way African Americans were feeling during the '60s. Many soul hits, such as Franklin's "Respect" and Brown's "Say It Loud, I'm Black and I'm Proud," were calls for recognition and independence.

Soul music had its share of important contributions from other singers influenced by gospel, such as Otis Redding, Wilson Pickett, the Staple Singers, and Sam and Dave. The Motown sound, a happy and upbeat form of soul from Detroit, Michigan, made a huge impact with many hit records. From the 1960s to the mid-1980s, recording acts such as the Temptations, the Supremes, Stevie Wonder, the Four Tops, and the Jackson Five made Motown a house-hold name. Motown was the largest and most successful record company ever owned by an African American. His name was Berry Gordy.

During the 1970s, soul continued to gain popularity with a smoother sound. Strings and complex arrangements were major parts of songs written and recorded by Barry White and by Kenny Gamble and Leon Huff (who created a style called The Sound of Philadelphia). The late 1970s, the 1980s, and the 1990s saw a return to a more gospel-influenced style of music. Groups like the O'Jays, Harold Melvin and the Blue Notes, and Guy featured lead singers whose strong voices reflected their gospel upbringing.

The Supremes © Bettman/CC

The **tambourine,** an important instrument in blues, gospel, and soul music, makes a wonderful sound. With metal disks attached to a small drum's frame, it sounds as if handclaps and cymbals are being played at the same time. Although the word *tambourine* refers to a European frame drum (a drum with a circular frame) that was played as early as the fourteenth century, the word is used to refer to all frame drums. Various kinds of tambourines were played in North America, Central Asia, Mesopotamia, and Egypt. In this activity, you will find that the tambourine is as easy to make as it is to play.

Tambourine

Here's What You Need

- one-hole paper punch
- sturdy aluminum pie pan
- ruler
- 2 sheets of white paper
- pencil
- scissors
- 8 small objects that will make noise when they hit the pan, such as paper clips, keys, and small bells
- 10 metal wire twists
- 2 pieces of ribbon about 8 inches (20 cm) long
- glue

Here's What You Do

1 Using the paper punch, make 10 holes around the edge of the pie pan that are about 1½ inches (4 cm) apart.

2 Place the pie pan facedown and put a sheet of paper on top of it. With the pencil, trace around the small circle in the center of the pan, then cut the circle out. Do the same with the second sheet of paper. With your markers, draw a pattern or design on one side of each paper circle. These circles will be used to decorate the front and back of your tambourine.

4 To add additional color and pizzazz to the instrument, thread the ribbons through the remaining holes.

5 For the finishing touch, put several drops of glue on the blank side of each paper circle you decorated. Glue one circle to the inside of the pie pan and the other to the outside of the pan. Allow the glue to dry for several minutes, then call a few friends and have your own jam session!

3 Secure each object (paper clips, keys, etc.) to the pan by threading a metal wire twist through the object and then through one of the holes in the pan. Use two or more twists to attach heavier objects like keys. Leave two of the holes empty.

Jazz

Jazz has been called the only classical form of music developed in the United States. A big part of jazz music, especially when played live, is improvisation. This is when musicians play the basic chords and structure of a song, then take turns doing solos that are variations of the song's melody. This gives musicians a chance to be creative.

Jazz was preceded by ragtime, a musical style that featured complex rhythm patterns played on the piano. Ragtime musicians such as Eubie Blake, Jelly Roll Morton, and Scott Joplin were known for playing popular songs and show tunes in a lighthearted, upbeat manner.

Jazz became popular in the early twentieth century, particularly in New Orleans, Chicago, and Memphis. Clarinetist-saxophonist Sidney Bechet and trumpeter-singer Louis Armstrong were just two of the musicians to gain popularity through the New Orleans jazz scene. It wasn't until 1923 that the first African American New Orleans–style jazz records were made.

Small jazz ensembles, and later big bands, made horn sections a central part of the music. The big bands, which sometimes had as many as fifteen horn players, a pianist, a drummer, and a vocalist, performed in large

Miles Davis. © *Mosaic Images*/CORBIS

dance halls. Many popular female jazz singers, such as Ella Fitzgerald and Sarah Vaughan, got their start in big bands. The piano became especially popular with later jazz musicians, such as Duke Ellington, Thelonious Monk, Count Basie, and Art Tatum.

Jazz is always changing and developing. Swing, big band, straight ahead, cool, acid, modal, and contemporary jazz styles were developed over the twentieth century. During the 1940s, several musicians gained recognition for creating bebop (or just bop), a style that was very different from anything anyone had ever heard. Bebop wasn't embraced by everyone because the musicians used odd rhythms, strange combinations of notes, and complex improvisations. Horn players Dizzy Gillespie and Charlie Parker were its main creators. Pianists Thelonious Monk and Bud Powell and bass player Charles Mingus are also credited with developing the style.

Trumpeter Miles Davis, also a part of the bebop era, made jazz exciting by constantly coming up with new ways to play the music. Miles was a primary creator of cool jazz, a more relaxed style of music that had complex harmonies and sometimes included French horns and tubas—

instruments that weren't often used in jazz. Later in his career, Davis was part of a trend called hard bop and created fusion, a music that combines jazz with various types of music, such as rock.

Today, jazz has come a long way from its early beginnings when musicians were limited to playing in small clubs and segregated dance halls. Now it is studied in universities and performed in concert halls around the world.

Since horn and wind instruments are important to jazz music, you might like to try to make your own version of a wind instrument. You'll need an adult's help for this activity. When you're done, play a little jazz number for your family and friends!

PASSING THE TORCH

Many of today's popular jazz musicians, such as Terence Blanchard, John Hicks, and Wynton Marsalis, got some of their formal music training in the classroom. These musicians also learned a lot about jazz music (its history and performance) by playing in the bands of drummer Art Blakey and vocalist Betty Carter, two innovative jazz artists who were intent on sharing their talent and knowledge. The pair used their ensembles as a training ground to teach young pianists, horn players, bassists, and drummers how to play in the true tradition of jazz. By being allowed to perform with Blakey and Carter in some of the most renowned jazz clubs around the world, many young musicians learned firsthand the ABCs of improvisation, how to play a variety of jazz styles, and the best way to present themselves (as performers) in front of a live audience.

Blakey, who was born in Pittsburgh, Pennsylvania, used his group the Jazz Messengers to feature upcoming musicians from 1954 until his death in 1990. Carter, known as godmother to several jazz players, was born in Flint, Michigan. She was credited with founding "Jazz Ahead," a music program that brought aspiring musicians to New York to play jazz. Carter died in 1998.

Wind Instrument

Here's What You Need

- tube of bamboo wood at least 12 inches (30 cm) long
- clean, soft cloth
- drill with a $3/16$-inch bit (about a $4^3/4$-mm) (requires adult help)
- ruler
- sandpaper
- adult helper

Here's What You Do

1 Wipe the tube of wood thoroughly with a piece of cloth before you begin.

2 Ask an adult to help you drill several holes in the wood using the $3/16$-inch bit. Drill the first hole $1^1/2$ inches (4 cm) from the end of the tube of wood. Be sure not to drill the hole all the way through the tube.

3 Measure 4 inches (10 cm) down from the first hole. Starting at that point, drill four holes that are 1 inch (2.5 cm) apart. These are your finger holes. You can create different pitches in sound by taking your fingers on and off these holes. (Feel free to drill the holes closer or farther apart for spacing that is comfortable for your fingers.)

4 When you've made the holes, there may be several rough edges. Use a small sheet of sandpaper to smooth the edges. Now you're ready to play away!

Rap

Syncopated (having strong accents placed on specific beats) words and rhythms. Poetry set to music. That's how rap can be described. Also known as hip-hop, rap was first developed around the early 1970s. While rap is the name given to the style of music, the term hip-hop represents rap culture—from the style of clothes rappers wear, to break dancing, beat boxing, and the slang rappers use when speaking.

Rap's influences go all the way back to Africa. African **griots** (storytellers) went from village to village carrying messages, telling tales, and commenting about life. Because part of a griot's job was to hold the audience's attention, these storytellers had to be exciting, musical, and have a special way with words. Rap also owes credit to the call-and-response tradition in gospel music. For example, a rapper might shout, "Everybody in the house say *ho*!" and the audience would respond, "Ho!"

Before rap became a popular musical style, there were African American musicians such as Gil Scott Heron and James Brown who were known for occasionally "rapping" over their music. James Brown is still probably one of the most sampled artists in rap history. (Sampling means to take a small portion of a recorded song and make it a part of your song or record.)

The island of Jamaica, known for its musical contribution of reggae, is where the basic elements of rap began. Rap deejays, or selectors, traveled around in flatbed trucks play-ing music and making their own movable parties. The trucks were loaded with turntables, large speakers, a microphone, and a generator, and the deejays would use this equipment to play loud instrumental versions of their favorite reggae tunes. To get the crowd involved, the deejays would also act as a

ROOTS, ROCK, REGGAE

Reggae music had quite an evolution before it gained worldwide popularity in the 1970s. After World War II, Jamaica was self-governed but still a member of the British Commonwealth. Jamaica's newfound independence helped spawn ska, an upbeat music that reflected Jamaicans' hope and joy for a better future. By the 1960s, ska had become less popular and musicians were beginning to play music with a slower, more constant beat. This style became known as rock steady. Although several musicians claimed to have been the first to record rock steady records, the style didn't become hugely popular until it evolved into reggae. Reggae advanced the sound of the music with recording-studio technology. The most popular artists to make reggae music were Bob Marley and the members of his group, the Wailers. They were a great influence on reggae artists around the globe who continue to make records today.

rapper and begin toasting (a Jamaican term that means rapping) over the music. In Jamaica, I-Roy, U-Roy and Prince Far-I were popular toasters. Today, this style of rap is known as dance hall.

During the 1970s, a young Jamaican deejay by the name of Kool Herc and his friend, DJ Hollywood, began playing records at parties in the Bronx, New York, and rapping or talking over them.

Kool Herc was known for using two turntables. He played two songs at the same time or faded one song into another. This technique came to be called mixing. The craze caught on around New York, and deejays and rappers began springing up all over. At first, rap was something people just did at parties and in clubs. But in 1979, a New Jersey rap group called the Sugar Hill Gang released a recording of the song "Rapper's Delight," which became a nationwide hit. That record was soon followed by Curtis Blow's "These Are the Breaks." Both records sold more than 500,000 copies, bringing rap music to the masses. Other rappers who are credited with helping shape rap music are Afrika Bambaataa, Grand Master Flash, LL Cool J, and Run-D.M.C. Originally a music of the clubs and streets, rap has become a multimillion-dollar business.

Most rappers rap about the things they like or don't like, or just things that happen to them. You can, too. Choose a subject, like something fun that happened to you recently, then create a rhyme. While you're at it, ask for a little help from a friend.

Write a Rap

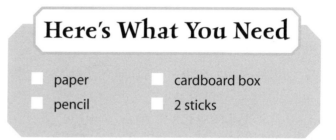

Here's What You Need

- [ ] paper
- [ ] pencil
- [ ] cardboard box
- [ ] 2 sticks

Here's What You Do

1 After you've chosen a subject to write about, begin writing your rap. Most raps follow a pattern that is similar to many other song lyrics, with several verses and a rhyming pattern. For your first rap, you'll write two verses and then something that is called a "hook." Each verse should be four lines and the words at the end of each pair of lines should rhyme. Here's a sample:

The weekend's here. It's time to do the chores.
I've got to wash the dishes and sweep the floors.
Just like a banker or a grocery store clerk,
I've got to change my clothes and get right to work!

2 Now on to the hook. The hook is the part of a rap that is repeated over and over. It's the "catchy" part of the song.

In most cases, a hook can be as little as one or as many as four lines. For example:

Well, my friends, now that school is through,
It's time to get busy, there's housework to do.
It's time to get busy, there's housework to do.

3 Grab paper and a pencil and write two verses of your own, then add a hook. When you're done, ask a friend to act as your drummer. Using the bottom of the cardboard box and a stick, the drummer should keep time by repeatedly hitting the box with four beats. Now recite your rhyme over the beat. If you'd like, write two more verses, then recite them in front of an audience.

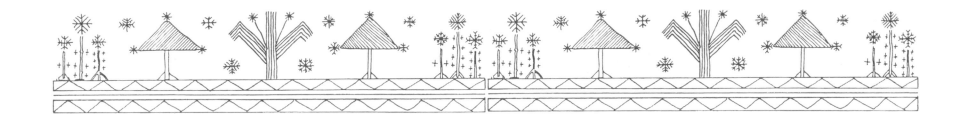

Dance

> "This company shows that there are Black dancers with the physique, temperament and stamina, and everything else it takes to produce what we call the 'born' ballet dancer."
>
> ARTHUR MITCHELL,
> FOUNDER, DANCE THEATER OF HARLEM

> "I learned in an environment that really respected tap as an art form. I was fortunate to be mentored by 'Bubber' Gaines, a tap legend. There was always tap being taught in the dance schools. But as a technique with training behind it taught by real master artists, you had to go into New York City. That's where things were really happening."
>
> DEBORAH MITCHELL,
> FOUNDER, NEW JERSEY TAP ENSEMBLE

People of all cultures have always enjoyed dancing for fun and to entertain others, but dance is also a way for people to express themselves. Historians have recorded that a distinct form of African American dancing began to develop as far back as the 1500s. It was during that time that the basic elements of **tap dancing** (dance performed wearing shoes with metal taps) and **jigging** (where a dancer overemphasized the movement of his or her hips, legs, and feet) were born.

From the late 1700s to mid-1800s, white dancers performed their own interpretations of African American song and dance styles, wearing their faces painted black. These performances, known as **minstrel shows,** (shows that depicted African Americans in an unflattering way) were extremely popular. Soon after the Civil War, African American dancers were allowed to perform in minstrel shows. They weren't happy about the negative depiction of their race, but participating in minstrel shows was the only way many African American dancers could get work.

By the late 1800s, touring road shows featured African American dancers in **vaudeville** (variety) shows where they were able to perform their own, less stereotypical, dance routines. It was during the vaudeville era that tap dancing got its start. By the 1920s, some vaudeville dancers who had spent their careers dancing in small clubs were starring in Hollywood films.

More than thirty years later, African American dancers who wanted to show they could also do other forms of dance, such as modern and ballet, were running into some of the same problems as their forebears. But the opportunities became much easier when two men, Alvin Ailey and Arthur Mitchell, started their own African American dance companies. Their troupes became important not just to African American dance but to American dance as it is known around the world.

Contemporary and Ballet Dancing

African Americans who wanted to dance in professional companies during the mid-1900s found it very difficult. Many aspiring dancers took lessons with some of the top teachers around the country. But when it came to auditioning to perform with major companies, especially ballet companies, they were turned down—and were often told their bodies didn't suit that type of dancing. Fortunately, things gradually began to change.

In 1954, Alvin Ailey, a native of Rogers, Texas, made his way to New York from Los Angeles. In New York, he got the opportunity to perform on Broadway, then later studied modern dance and ballet with Charles Weidman and Martha Graham. In 1958, he decided to start his own company with just seven dancers. The Alvin Ailey American Dance Theater started by performing standard modern dances and newer works created by Ailey and other aspiring choreographers.

For the next few years, the company would attract a great deal of attention by performing modern dances that had African American life as the theme. One of the company's most popular dances, which Ailey created in 1960, was "Revelations." Performed to several traditional gospel songs in which dancers re-create a baptism, conduct a group prayer, and rejoice in a joyous celebration, "Revelations" is still one of their most popular ballets. Other popular Ailey dances include "Cry" and "The Stack-Up."

By the 1960s, the company had performed as far away as France, Australia, Africa, the Netherlands, and Brazil. Ailey had also broken new ground by choreographing dances for the Joffrey Ballet and the American Ballet Theatre. In 1969, Ailey opened a school for dancers. Later, in 1974, he started the Alvin Ailey Repertory Ensemble. The Alvin Ailey Student Performance Group, which was formed in 1984, gives young dancers the opportunity to perform professionally.

Meanwhile, in 1955, Arthur Mitchell became the first African American man to dance for a major ballet company. In 1969, Mitchell created the Dance Theater of Harlem (DTH) with Karel Shook, a white dance teacher. They

PIONEERING AFRICAN AMERICAN DANCE

Before Arthur Mitchell and Alvin Ailey began making lasting impressions on the world of dance, an African American woman named Katherine Dunham paved the way with many groundbreaking accomplishments. An anthropologist who studied at the University of Chicago, Dunham was also an influential dancer and choreographer. She was known for incorporating Caribbean and African movements into her dances; her dance technique also focused on moving specific body parts in a different manner than the rest of the body.

In 1940, Dunham started the highly acclaimed Katherine Dunham Dance Company, which performed in more than fifty countries. In 1943, the Katherine Dunham School of Arts and Research was established. Until the mid-1960s, the school trained dancers in African and Caribbean dance and classical ballet. One of her most famous students was Arthur Mitchell, founder of the Dance Theater of Harlem.

In 1964, Dunham became the first African American to choreograph a work (Verdi's *Aida*) for New York's Metropolitan Opera. She also performed in and choreographed Broadway musicals and a number of motion pictures, including *Stormy Weather*, which starred Lena Horne. The first and most revered figure in African American dance, Katherine Dunham set a standard of excellence for African American choreographers and dancers to follow.

Arthur Mitchell (center), a dancer and the founder of the dance Theater of Harlem dance and music school, shown here with students. © *Bettman/CC.*

originally created DTH as a dance school, but out of the school grew a mostly African American ballet company. The DTH gave its first major performance in 1971, after which Mitchell and his troupe began touring the world, performing in England, South Africa, and Russia. Today, DTH continues to give youngsters in the Harlem community a chance to learn ballet and choreography. It also has more than thirty dancers that continue to tour the world and perform special programs.

Of course, professional dancers who belong to companies spend years learning how to dance. But learning some of the basic "positions" of ballet is easy. So, put on your dancin' shoes and give it a try.

Ballet Steps

Here's What You Need

☐ space to dance

☐ full-length mirror

☐ stereo (optional)

Here's What You Do

1 Stand in front of the mirror before you begin. To stand in the "first position" of ballet, put your feet together, with your toes pointed outward and the back of your heels touching. Hold your arms out and slightly downward. Be sure that your hands are pointed toward each other so that your arms make an oval shape.

First position   Second position   Third position   Fourth position   Fifth position

2 In the "second position," stand with your feet apart, still pointing outward. Stretch your arms and hands out at your sides. Hold your arms as straight as possible.

3 In the "third position," bring your feet back together, placing the heel of one foot against the arch of the other. Extend your arms forward again as in the first position to create a large circle. But this time, don't point your hands toward each other.

4 For the "fourth position," move the foot that was pressed against the arch (the foot in front) slightly forward so that the two feet are parallel. Next, bring one arm up over your head and leave the other arm extended outward.

5 The "fifth position" is a little difficult, so don't be discouraged if you can't quite do it. Place one foot behind the other. Now try to bring both feet together, facing them in opposite directions, so that they touch. Now bring both arms up over your head to create a big oval shape.

6 Now go through all the positions again. Remember to keep your body straight and tall. This time, put on some soft music. Once you've mastered these positions, you can try adding a few spins and leaps.

Tap

Tap dancers' shoes are like a set of drums. Every part—the heel, the toe, and the inner and outer soles—is used to create clicking, clunking, slapping, pounding, and tapping sounds. They tap softly, loudly, quickly, and slowly. Tap dancers do it all!

Originally, tap dancers made up all of their own moves. But by the early 1900s, tap had basic dance steps everyone knew, such as the time step, which was made up of a specific combination of steps such as the shuffle, slap, ball, heel, or stamp. Unlike other dance forms, such as ballet, early tap dancers didn't learn their craft through formal training. They learned by watching other dancers in clubs or on street corners. They copied each other's steps, then sometimes changed a step or two to make the dance their own.

Early tap dancers didn't have the metal plates attached to their shoes that tappers have today. Instead, they laid boards across barrels and danced on them to create sounds, or danced in wooden clogs. The tradition of creating swishing and shuffling noises by dancing on sand thrown over a board was created well before the 1900s. Tappers still use that technique today.

By the 1920s, tap-dancing acts that had gotten their start in vaudeville started performing in Broadway shows. Vaudeville veteran Bill "Bojangles" Robinson was an important tap dance figure of the period. In addition to dancing on Broadway, he appeared in many films dancing with Shirley Temple during the '30s and '40s. The Nicholas Brothers, a two-brother dance team who added flips and splits to their dance routines, were also big movie attractions. Cholly Atkins, Charles "Honi" Coles, and Howard "Sandman" Simms were also important to the development of tap. After learning everything they could about the art form, they taught tap dancing to many young dancers who later went on to appear in Broadway shows.

As popular as tap had become in the first half of the twentieth century, people seemed to lose interest in it by the 1950s, when they turned their attention to other forms of dance. But tap dancing became popular again in the 1980s with the Broadway play *Sophisticated Ladies,* featuring Gregory Hines. The film world contributed to tap's resurgence with the release of the movie *Tap*. The film starred Hines, Sammy Davis Jr., and a young tap sensation, Savion Glover. Today, young tappers are learning as much as they can from veteran dancers. They're also giving tap their own stamp by pairing it with rap and percussion sounds played on everything from tin cans to plastic barrels.

Have a little fun making tap sounds with your very own tap shoes. Here's how!

Tap Shoes

Here's What You Need

- newspaper
- old pair of sneakers or shoes
- glue
- 10 pennies or quarters
- big wooden board
- sand or sugar

Here's What You Do

1 Spread several sheets of newspaper on the floor or on a table.

2 Take the sneakers or old shoes and turn them over so that the soles are facing upward. Apply three large drops of glue around the toe end of each sole. Be sure to leave a little space in between the drops.

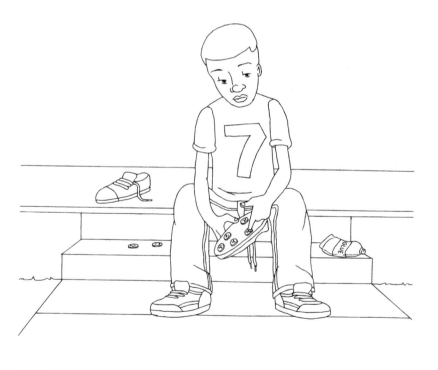

3 Place a coin over each drop of glue and press the coin down. Allow the glue to dry.

4 Put two drops of glue on the heel of each sole and press a coin into each drop. Allow the glue to dry.

5 To try out your tap shoes, take the wooden board outside and place it on the ground. Try tapping loudly and softly on the board, sometimes using the toe of your shoe and then the heel to make different sounds. For a little added fun, pour a little sand or sugar onto the board and move the heel or toe of your shoe around in a twisting motion to create different sounds.

TAP DANCING TRADITION

Tap dancers frequently had challenges to see who could come up with the most exciting tap moves or sounds. Tappers still participate in tap challenges today.

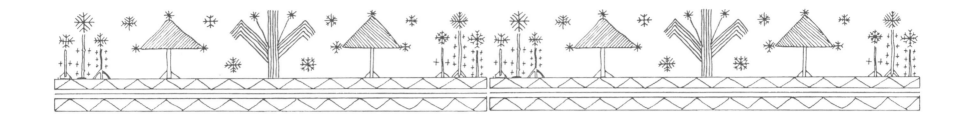

Literature

> " *When I read great literature, great drama, speeches, or sermons, I feel that the human mind has not achieved anything greater than the ability to share feelings and thoughts through language.* "
>
> JAMES EARL JONES, ACTOR

African American literature has come a long way since the seventeenth and eighteenth centuries, when most African Americans were denied the opportunity to learn to read or write. But that kind of oppression could not last long. African Americans nurtured their language and stories through the spoken word, and eventually had the opportunity to express themselves in writing. From the poems of Phyllis Wheatley in the eighteenth century to Walter Dean Myers' modern stories for young people, the literature of many African American writers is enjoyed by millions and taught in classrooms throughout the United States and around the world.

Phyllis Wheatley was the first African American writer to be published. Wheatley was born in Africa, but grew up as a slave in Boston. Her situation was different from that of most slaves. Her owners encouraged her to read and write. Her first book of poems, published in 1773, was the second book of poetry published by an American woman of any race.

Some of the earliest writings by African Americans were called **slave narratives** (writings that described the lives the slaves lived, how they coped with adversity, and the kind of lives they hoped their children would have). Important slave narratives were written by Frederick Douglass, an anti-slave leader, and Olaudah Equiano, a slave born in Africa.

By the early 1900s, African American writers felt comfortable enough to write about other issues that were also important to them. One of the most important books printed during that time was *The Souls of Black Folk* by W. E. B. DuBois, which was published in 1903. The book discussed the role of African Americans in America up until that point and the importance of doing away with racism.

An important era in African American writing was the 1920s and 1930s. It was called the **Harlem Renaissance** (a time when many writers, musicians, and artists who had made their way to the North congregated in Harlem, a mostly black section of New York City, to create art). In the space of a few years, these artists wrote and published a vast amount of work that changed the way both whites and blacks thought about African American life and culture. Poets Langston Hughes, Sterling A. Brown, Arna Bontemps, and Countee

FAMOUS WORKS OF THE HARLEM RENAISSANCE

God Sends Sunday by Arna Bontemps (novel)

The Weary Blues by Langston Hughes (poetry)

Not without Laughter by Langston Hughes (novel)

Their Eyes Were Watching God by Zora Neale Hurston (novel)

Cane by Jean Toomer (short stories and poetry)

Harlem Shadows by Claude McKay (poetry)

The Autobiography of an Ex–Colored Man by James Weldon Johnson (novel)

Cullen and writers Claude McKay, Richard Wright, and Zora Neale Hurston all came out of the Harlem Renaissance. Although the creativity that marked the Harlem Renaissance faded with the Great Depression, the 1950s brought the world the amazing talent of Ralph Ellison. His classic book *Invisible Man* vividly describes the life of a young black man struggling with racial prejudice in mid-twentieth century America.

James Baldwin, one of the most popular African American authors, got his start writing essays in the late 1940s. He went on to write both fiction and nonfiction about the lives of

African Americans. Baldwin was also deeply involved in the Civil Rights Movement, giving lectures at colleges and participating in marches. Among his many books are *Go Tell It on the Mountain* and *Another Country*. As Richard Wright had done earlier, Baldwin spent much of his life writing in other parts of the world, where he found life as a black man and artist much easier.

Author James Baldwin. © *Bettmann*/CORBIS.

AFRICAN AMERICAN NEWSPAPERS AND MAGAZINES

Freedom's Journal was the first African American newspaper. It was established in New York City in 1827 by Samuel E. Cornish and John B. Russwurm to discuss slavery and citizenship for African Americans. By the mid–nineteenth century, newspapers were also being published in Pittsburgh, Pennsylvania, and Cleveland, Ohio. And by the Civil War, nearly forty African American newspapers were being published. After the war, an estimated 575 African American newspapers had been established. Many did not survive, but the *Philadelphia Tribune* (founded in 1884) and the *Amsterdam News* (established in New York City in 1909) were among those that flourished. The *Tribune* was published well into the 1990s and the *Amsterdam News* continues to be published today.

The *Crisis,* the first African American magazine, was started in 1910 by W. E. B. Du Bois. It was the official magazine of the National Association for the Advancement of Colored People (NAACP). Like other magazines that followed, the *Crisis* focused on commentaries about race relations and racial progress instead of news. The first magazine to focus on African American news and consumer information was the *Negro Digest,* created in the early 1940s by John H. Johnson. In 1946, Johnson established *Ebony* magazine, which focused on consumer information and entertainment. The Johnson publishing empire, which also published *Jet* and *Ebony Man* magazines, led the way for other African American–owned magazines, including *Essence, Black Enterprise,* and Oprah Winfrey's *O* magazine.

During the Black Arts movement of the 1960s, African American playwrights such as Lorraine Hansberry and Leroi Jones (also known as Amiri Baraka) were gaining popularity. During the 1970s, African American women writers began to get increased attention. Most recognized were Maya Angelou, whose *I Know Why the Caged Bird Sings,* the story of the author's childhood in the south, is still a best-seller thirty years after it was first published; Alice Walker, whose novel *The Color Purple* won the Pulitzer Prize and the National Book Award and was made into a motion picture; and Toni Morrison, author of the Pulitzer Prize–winning *Beloved* and many other works, who in 1993 became the first African American woman to receive the Nobel Prize for Literature.

Keeping a daily journal is a good way to jot down ideas that could one day become a poem or story. Why not make a journal of your own?

Journal

Here's What You Need

- 8 sheets of white 8$\frac{1}{2}$-by-11-inch (2$\frac{1}{2}$-by-28-cm) paper
- scissors
- ruler
- 1 sheet of light-colored 8$\frac{1}{2}$-by-11-inch (21$\frac{1}{2}$-by-28-cm) construction paper
- one-hole paper punch
- colored markers
- four 6-inch (15-cm) pieces of yarn

Here's What You Do

1 To make the pages for your journal, fold all of the sheets of white paper in half lengthwise. Cut the pages along the fold. You should now have 16 sheets of paper that measure 8$\frac{1}{2}$ by 5$\frac{1}{2}$ inches (22 by 14 cm). Fold and cut your construction paper to the same measurements. You should now have two pieces of colored paper.

2 Using the paper punch, make four holes along one side of all of the sheets of paper. Starting 1 inch (2.5 cm) from the top left corner, make the holes 2 inches (5 cm) apart.

3 Use the markers to decorate one of the sheets of construction paper. Draw a pattern or simply write your name. This will be the front cover of your journal.

4 When you're done with the cover, stack all of the remaining pages together, putting the other page of colored construction paper on the bottom. String a piece of yarn through each hole and tie it tightly. Now that your book is done, keep a journal of the things that happen to you every day or start your own short story. Add additional pages whenever you like.

VI
SOUL FOOD AND CARIBBEAN CUISINE

"We were not a rich family, so we learned how to use leftovers and stretch them. We also had a garden, so it wasn't uncommon for us to grow our own tomatoes and peppers. I was taught to utilize the things we had.

JOE BROWN, SOUL FOOD CHEF AND RESTAURANT OWNER

Soul food is the name that was affectionately given to African American cooking sometime during the late 1960s or early 1970s. It was given the name because of the loving care that was taken while it was being prepared. The word *soul* reflected the social consciousness of the time and also described the wonderful way families felt when they sat down to eat.

Soul food, which was once called down-home food and country food, got its start on Southern plantations. Slaves used the ingredients that were most readily available to create flavorful foods. They used vegetables such as collard, turnip, and mustard greens. Since there was an abundance of pigs on the plantations, pork became a big part of Southern cooking. It was used to add flavor to bitter greens and to make ham, spare ribs, and pork chops.

Side dishes of corn bread, hoe cake (a large, pancake-like biscuit), and biscuits helped to stretch portions when other foods weren't available. Over the years, other popular soul food dishes came to include macaroni and cheese, fried chicken, potato salad, and sweet potato pie. Today, because many people are concerned with the health value of the foods they eat, soul food is often cooked with low-fat ingredients.

Caribbean cuisine is also a favorite of African Americans. Dishes such as rice and peas, jerk chicken (chicken made with "jerk," a spicy Caribbean seasoning), akee (a fruit that grows in the tropics) and salt fish (codfish), red snapper, and plantain got their origin on Caribbean islands, such as Jamaica, Trinidad, and Guyana. Caribbean cuisine became popular in the United States during the early 1990s.

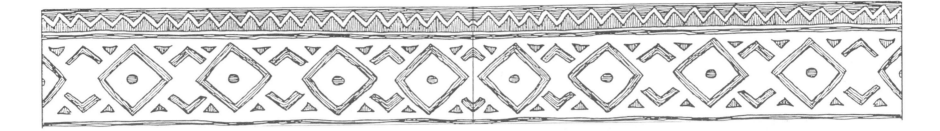

Corn Bread and Biscuits

Corn bread is a staple of African American cooking. It was first made, though, by Native Americans. Made with salt, cornmeal, and water, the earliest corn breads were called *pone.* Years later, corn breads were made differently in the North and the South. People living in Northern states used a great deal of flour and sugar while Southerners didn't use either ingredient. For a taste of homemade corn bread and biscuits, try making them using these tasty recipes. (For a lower fat content, substitute light margarine and 2% milk for the butter and buttermilk.)

Corn Bread

Here's What You Need

SERVES: 6–8
Recipe requires adult help.

Ingredients

- ☐ 2 cups (480 mL) self-rising white cornmeal
- ☐ 2 tablespoons (30 mL) sugar
- ☐ ½ teaspoon (2 mL) baking soda
- ☐ 1 large egg
- ☐ 1½ cups (360 mL) buttermilk
- ☐ 3 tablespoons (45 mL) butter or shortening
- ☐ butter
- ☐ jam or jelly

Equipment

- ☐ measuring cup
- ☐ measuring spoons
- ☐ large bowl
- ☐ large wooden spoon
- ☐ small bowl
- ☐ small spoon
- ☐ small frying pan
- ☐ square 8-inch (20-cm) baking pan
- ☐ oven mitts
- ☐ toothpicks
- ☐ butter knife

Here's What You Do

1 Preheat the oven to 425°F (170°C).

2 Pour the cornmeal, sugar, and baking soda into the large bowl and mix with the wooden spoon. Set the bowl aside while you prepare the other ingredients.

3 Beat the egg in the small bowl for about 30 seconds with the small spoon. Then pour the egg into the large bowl.

4 Slowly pour the buttermilk into the large bowl while stirring with the wooden spoon. When all of the milk is in the mixture, stir well.

5 Ask an adult to help you melt the butter or shortening in the frying pan. Melt the butter over a low flame. Once it has melted, ask an adult to use some of it to coat the bottom of your baking pan. Then pour the remaining melted butter or shortening into the mixture in the large bowl. Using the wooden spoon, stir the butter or shortening into the other ingredients.

6 Pour the corn bread mix into the baking pan.

7 Bake the corn bread for 20 to 25 minutes. Have an adult take it out of the oven using oven mitts. To make sure it's done, poke a toothpick in the center. If it comes out completely clean, then the corn bread is done. If it has a little corn bread mix on it, cook it for another 5 minutes or until a toothpick comes out clean.

8 Let the corn bread cool for 15 minutes. Cut it into medium-sized squares with the butter knife, and serve with butter and jam, or jelly. Enjoy!

SOUL FOOD TRADITION

Although soul food dishes can be eaten anytime, they are traditionally cooked and served at family gatherings, holidays, and other special occasions. It is customary for family members or friends to bring their specialty dish to the host's home to share with the other family members or guests.

Biscuits

Here's What You Need

SERVINGS: 16 BISCUITS
Recipe requires adult help.

Ingredients

- [ ] 2 cups (480 mL) self-rising flour plus a little extra
- [ ] ½ cup (120 mL) Crisco shortening (solid)
- [ ] ⅔ to ¾ (160 to 180 mL) cup of milk
- [ ] 1 tablespoon (15 mL) butter or magarine
- [ ] jam or jelly

Equipment

- [ ] measuring cup
- [ ] large bowl
- [ ] fork
- [ ] large wooden spoon
- [ ] waxed paper
- [ ] rolling pin
- [ ] 2-inch (5-cm) biscuit cutter
- [ ] large baking sheet
- [ ] measuring spoon
- [ ] small frying pan
- [ ] pastry or basting brush

Here's What You Do

1 Preheat the oven to 450°F (200°C).

2 Put the 2 cups (480 mL) of flour in the large bowl, then add the shortening. Using the fork, mash the shortening into the flour until the mixture looks like fine crumbs.

3 Slowly pour in the milk and stir with the wooden spoon until a soft dough forms. You may or may not need to use all of the milk.

4 Place the dough on a sheet of lightly floured waxed paper. Using your palms and knuckles, knead (press, pat and roll) the dough for several minutes. Use the rolling pin to flatten the dough until it is ½ inch (1.3 cm) thick.

5 Lightly flour the biscuit cutter. Press the cutter into the dough to create 2-inch (5-cm) dough circles. Place each dough circle on an ungreased baking sheet. Be sure that the sides of the circles are touching. This will make the edges less crunchy when baked.

6 Bake the biscuits for 10 to 12 minutes or until they are golden brown. With an adult's help, melt 1 tablespoon (15 mL) of butter in a small frying pan. When the biscuits are done, brush the top of each with a small amount of melted butter or margarine. Serve with jam or jelly.

Fried Plantain

Plantain is a banana-like fruit that grows in the tropics. A popular Caribbean and Hispanic food, it is enjoyed by people all over the world. Plantains are different from bananas because they must be cooked before they can be eaten. If a plantain is cooked while it is still green, it will taste similar to squash or potato. As a plantain ripens, it turns yellow and then blackens. When this happens, it becomes softer and has a sweeter taste. Fried plantain tastes great with meats or on its own.

CENTERPIECES TO CARIBBEAN CUISINE

Fruits, breads, and vegetables are important staples in Caribbean cooking. Tropical fruits such as plantain, mango, avocado, pineapple, coconut, and papaya are used to make a variety of pies, sauces, juices, pastries, and milk. Callaloo, or taro root leaves, is a popular Caribbean vegetable that was originally brought to the Caribbean from Africa in the seventeenth century. It is similar in texture to collard greens, a traditional African American vegetable. Breads such as hard dough bread (a white bread), coco bread (also known as coconut bread, a rich bread often eaten with beef patties), and bullah (a type of gingerbread) act as great side additions to many Caribbean dishes.

Here's What You Need

Serves: 3
Recipe requires adult help.

Ingredients

- 2 large plantains
- 5 tablespoons (74 mL) corn oil

Equipment

- cutting board
- butter knife
- frying pan
- metal tongs
- metal spatula
- paper plate
- paper towels

Here's What You Do

1 Peel both plantains, then place them on the cutting board. Using the butter knife, cut each plantain at an angle into long, oval pieces.

2 Cover the bottom of the frying pan with the corn oil. Ask an adult to heat the pan on medium until the oil is hot. Use the metal tongs to place several pieces of plantain into the pan. In a few minutes, when the pieces are lightly browned, flip them over with the spatula and allow the other side to lightly brown.

4 Cover the plate with a paper towel, then place the cooked plantain pieces on the plate. To remove excess oil, pat the tops of the plantain pieces with another paper towel.

5 Repeat steps 3 and 4 until you've cooked all the plantain pieces. Allow them to cool, and invite a few friends over for a little taste testing.

Glossary

adire   tie-dyed fabrics made by the Yoruba people of Nigeria.

appliqué   a technique that involves stitching patterns of cutout fabric on a solid background

badima   a pedestal-based drum used in funerals.

calabash   a hard-shelled fruit that grows in the tropics.

civil rights   the rights of citizens to equality and political and social freedom.

conga drum   a drum played by hand that is used in Latin and African American music.

cornrowing   braiding hair close to the scalp.

culture   the artistic and ethnic customs of a group of people.

cylindrical   shaped like or made of a hollow body with straight sides and a flat round top and bottom.

desegregation   abolition of racial segregation.

dreadlocks   hair twisted into matted braids.

emancipation   freedom from slavery.

embroidery   decorations created with a needle and thread.

griot   storyteller.

Harlem Renaissance   a period of time in the 1920s and 1930s when writers, musicians, and artists migrated to Harlem to create art.

hallowdays   elections and coronations observed by free blacks and slaves living in the North.

Imani   faith—to believe in God, yourself, your family, and others. One of the seven principles of Kwanzaa.

jigging   overemphasis of the movement of a dancer's hips, legs, and feet.

jook joint   a small shack-like club where musicians once played live music and people danced.

jubilee   a Southern form of gospel music that is rhythmically similar to the blues.

karamu   a special feast at Kwanzaa.

kettledrums   drums that are supported by wooden frames and played with sticks.

kikombe cha umoja   a symbolic cup also known as a **unity cup,** used at Kwanzaa.

kinara   a wooden candleholder used at Kwanzaa.

Kujichagulia   Self-determination—to work toward doing things that will strengthen your future. One of the seven principles of Kwanzaa.

Kuumba   Creativity—to use your talents to uplift others. One of the seven principles of Kwanzaa.

Kwanzaa   ("first fruits") the first African American cultural celebration or holiday.

mancala   a board game from Africa.

mankuntu   cylindrical drums that have various pitches.

masabe   a popular drum played by the Tonga people of Zambia.

mazao   fruits and vegetables used at Kwanzaa to represent the harvest and to symbolize the importance of working together.

minstrel shows   stage shows that presented African Americans in an unflattering way.

mishumma   seven candles of a kinara.

mkeka   a straw mat used at Kwanzaa.

muhindi   an ear of corn used at Kwanzaa to represent each child in the family.

muraburaba   a game from Lesotho.

musimbo   a popular drum played by the Tonga people of Zambia.

muslin   a woven cotton fabric.

Nia   Purpose—to work with others to make life better. One of the seven principles of Kwanzaa.

Nguzo Saba   the seven principles of Kwanzaa.

patchwork   using small pieces of cloth to make a pattern.

pilgrimage   a journey taken for sentimental reasons.

pone   corn bread made with salt, cornmeal, and water.

quilting   the craft of making quilts.

race records   songs recorded by African American musicians.

sampling   taking a portion of music from a recorded song and using it in a different song.

slave narrative   an early writing that described the life and thoughts of a slave.

syncopated having accents placed on certain beats or words.

tambourine a musical instrument consisting of a circular frame with metal disks attached to the inside.

tap dancing dance performed wearing shoes with metal taps.

Ujama Cooperative Economics—to develop jobs and businesses that benefit your family and the community. One of the seven principles of Kwanzaa.

Ujima Collective Work and Responsibility—to work together and to help others. One of the seven principles of Kwanzaa.

Umoja Unity—to build togetherness as a family, community, and nation. One of the seven principles of Kwanzaa.

unity cup see **kikombe cha umoja.**

vaudeville a variety show.

zawadi gifts given during Kwanzaa.

Index

A

acid, style of music, 81
activities
  ballet steps/positions,
    learning, 90–92
  biscuits, making, 105–6
  Black History Month
    banner, 12–13
  calabash, decorating, 44–45
  Chigoro Danda game, 70
  corn bread, making, 104–5
  cornrows, braiding, 31–34
  folktale, making your own,
    27–29
  fried plantains, making,
    107–8
  journal, making a, 98–99
  Juneteenth picnic basket,
    16
  Kwanzaa necklace, 20–21
  Little Sally Walker game, 65
  mancala game, 62–63

  Martin Luther King Jr.
    scroll, 8–9
  muraburaba game, 67–68
  quilting, 37–39
  rap, writing a, 85–86
  talking drum, 56–57
  tambourine, making,
    79–80
  tap dancing, 93–94
  tribal mask, 51–52
  T-shirt, tie-dyeing, 47–49
  wind instrument, making,
    83
adire, 46–49, 109
a-fishing, 60
Africa, people of
  Ashanti kings, 59
  Bamabara, 53
  Bushongo, 61
  Marka, 53
  Nigerian, 49
  Tonga, 55
  Yoruba, 34, 46

Africa, regions, countries,
  and villages of, 23
  Benin, 40
  Central Africa, 36, 54, 55
  Congo, 55, 61
  East Africa, 46
  Gabon, 60
  Ghana, 55, 59, 60
  Kenya, 46
  Lesotho, 59, 66
  Liberia, 50
  Nigeria, 43, 46, 49, 50, 55
  South Africa, 66
  Tanzania, 46
  West Africa, 36, 40, 46, 61
  Yote, 59
  Zaire, 55
  Zambia, 55
  Zimbabwe, 60, 64, 69
Afrika Bambaataa, 85
Ailey, Alvin, 88–89
akee, as Caribbean cuisine,
  102

Alvin Ailey American Dance
  Theater, 88
Alvin Ailey Repertory
  Ensemble, 89
Alvin Ailey Student
  Performance Group, 89
American Ballet Theatre, 89
Amsterdam News, 97
Angelou, Maya, 98
Another Country (Baldwin),
  97
appliqué, 40, 109
Armstrong, Louis, 81
Asante, Molefi Kete, 10
Association for the Study of
  Negro Life and History, 11
Atkins, Cholly, 92
*Autobiography of an
  Ex-Colored Man, The*
  (Johnson), 96
avocado, as centerpiece to
  Caribbean cuisine, 107
awari. *See* mancala

B

badima, 55, 109
Baldwin, James, 96, 97
ballet steps, 90–92
  illustration of positions, 91
ball step, of tap, 92
banner for Black History
    Month, 12–13
Baraka, Amiri, 75, 98
barbecuing as popular
    Juneteenth tradition, 15
Basie, Count, 81
bebop, 81
Bechet, Sidney, 81
Beloved (Morrison), 98
Benin, appliqué technique
    from, 40
"Bible Quilt, The", 36
big band style of music, 81
Billboard magazine, 77
biscuits, 102, 105–6
  making, 105–6
Black Arts movement, 98
Black Enterprise magazine,
    97
Black History Month, 4,
    10–13
Blackburn, A. B., 11

Blake, Eubie, 81
Blakey, Art, 82
Blanchard, Terence, 82
Blow, Curtis, 85
blues, 75, 76–77
board game
  mancala, 62–63
  muraburaba, 67–68
Bontemps, Arna, 96
box braids, 30
Br'er (Bruh) Rabbit folktale,
    26
Broadway shows, 88, 89, 92,
    93
  Sophisticated Ladies, 93
Brown, James, 78, 84
Brown, Joe, 101
Brown, Sterling A., 96
bullah, as centerpiece to
    Caribbean cuisine, 107
bus boycott (Montgomery,
    Alabama), 6, 12
Bushongo tribe, 61

C

Caesar, Shirley, 77
calabash, 41, 43–45, 109
  decorating a, 44–45
  uses for, 43

callaloo, as centerpiece to
    Caribbean cuisine, 107
call-and-response singing,
    77, 78, 84
  rap and, 84
Cane (Toomer), 96
Caribbean cuisine, 102, 107–8
  centerpieces to, 107
  fried plantain, 107–8
Carter, Betty, 82
celebrations, African
    American, 3–21
  Black History Month, 4,
    10–13
  Juneteenth, 4, 14–17
  Kwanzaa, 4, 18–21
  Martin Luther King Jr. Day,
    4, 5–9
centerpieces to Caribbean
    cuisine, 107
Central Africa, 36, 54, 55
Central Asia, 79
Chicago, Illinois, 81
chicken, 19
  fried, as soul food, 102
Chigoro Danda, 60, 69–71
choreography, 89
civil rights, definition of, 6,
    109

Civil Rights movement, 6–7,
    77, 97
  songs for, 77
clothing
  as big part of African
    heritage, 41–42
  rap, 84
  ritual in early Juneteenth
    celebrations, 15
coco bread, as centerpiece to
    Caribbean cuisine, 107
coconut, as centerpiece to
    Caribbean cuisine, 107
Coles, Charles "Honi", 92
collard greens, 19, 102, 107
Color Purple, The (Walker),
    98
conga drums, 55, 109
Congo, 55, 61
contemporary dancing,
    88–90
Conyers, John, 7
cool, style of music, 81
corn braids, 30
corn bread, 102, 103–5
  making, 104–5
Cornish, Samuel E., 97
cornrowing, 31–34, 109
  creating, 31–33

styles of, 34
crafts, 41–57
  adire (tie-dyeing), 46–49
  calabash, 43–45
  drums, 54–57
  mask making, 50–53
Crisis magazine, 97
"Cry", 89
Cullen, Countee, 96
culture, African American,
    73–94, 109
  dance, 73, 87–94
  literature, 73, 95–99
  music, 73, 75–86
cylindrical, 55, 109

D

dance, 87–94
  ballet, 88–92
  contemporary, 88–90
  pioneering African
    American, 89
  tap dancing, 88, 92–94
dance hall style of rap, 85
Dance Theater of Harlem,
    87, 89–90
Davis, Miles, 81–82
Davis, Sammy Jr., 93
deejays, 84–85

desegregation, 6, 13, 109
Dixie Hummingbirds, 77
DJ Hollywood, 85
Douglass, Frederick, 11, 96
Downing, P. B., 13
dreadlocks, 31, 109
drums, 54–57
  badima, 55
  conga, 55
  dun–dun, 55
  kettledrum, 55
  making a, 56–57
  mankuntu, 55
  masabe, 55
  mushimbo, 55
  uses for, 54–55
DuBois, W. E. B., 96, 97
dun–dun drum, 55
Dunham, Katherine, 89

E

East Africa, 46
Ebony magazine, 97
Ebony Man magazine, 97
Edwards, Al, 15
Egypt
  games played in, 59, 61
  hair braiding in, 31
  tambourine in, 79

Ellington, Duke, 81
Ellison, Ralph, 96
emancipation, 15, 109
embroidery, 37, 109
Equiano, Olaudah, 96
Essence magazine, 97

F

Fitzgerald, Ella, 81
folktales, African American,
    24, 25–29
  Br'er Rabbit, 26
  making your own, 27–29
  "The Peculiar Such Thing",
    29
  "The People Could Fly", 29
  "The Wolf and Little
    Daughter", 26–27
follow-the-leader, 60
food
  biscuits recipe, 105–6
  Caribbean cuisine, 101–2,
    107–8
  corn bread recipe, 104–5
  fried plantain, 107–8
  of Juneteenth, 15
  of Kwanzaa, 19
  soul food, 101–6
Four Tops, 78

Franklin, Aretha, 77–78
Freedom's Journal, 97
French braids, 30
fusion music, 82

G

Gabon, 60
Gaines, "Bubber", 87
Galveston, Texas, 15, 17
  pilgrimage to, 17
Gamble, Kenny, 78
games, 59–71
  Chigoro Danda, 69–71
  Little Sally Walker, 64–65
  origins of, 59–60
  mancala, 61–63
  muraburaba, 66–68
Garvey, Marcus, 19
Ghana
  drums in, 55
  games in, 59, 60
Gillespie, Dizzy, 81
glossary, 109–11
Glover, Savion, 93
God Sends Sunday
    (Bontemps), 96
Gordy, Berry, 78
gospel, 76–77, 84–85
  influence on rap, 84–85

Go Tell It on the Mountain (Baldwin), 97
Graham, Martha, 88
Grand Master Flash, 85
Granger, Gordon, 14, 15
griot, 84, 109
Guy, 78
Guyana, food of, 102

H

hair braiding, 30–34
  cornrows, 31–33
Hair Raising: Beauty, Culture, and African American Women, 30
hairstyles worn by African Americans, 30–31
  box braids, 30
  corn braids, 30
  cornrows, 31
  dreadlocks, 31
  French braids, 30
hallowdays, 3, 109
Handy, W. C., 76
Hansberry, Lorraine, 98
hard bop, 82
hard dough bread, as centerpiece to Caribbean cuisine, 107

Harlem Renaissance, 96–97, 109
  famous works of the, 96
Harlem Shadows (McKay), 96
heel step, of tap, 92
Henry Ford Museum, 15
Herc, Kool, 85
Heron, Gil Scott, 84
Hicks, John, 82
Hines, Gregory, 93
hip-hop. *See* rap
hoe cake, as soul food, 102
hook, as part of rap song, 85–86
Hooker, John Lee, 77
"Hound Dog", 77
Horne, Lena, 89
Huff, Leon, 78
Hughes, Langston, 96
Hunter, Alberta, 76
Hurston, Zora Neale, 24, 96

I

"I Have a Dream" speech, 6
I Know Why the Caged Bird Sings (Angelou), 98
Imani, 19, 109

improvisation in music, 81, 82
Indigo dye, 49
instruments, musical
  clarinet, 81
  cymbals, 77
  drums, 55, 77
  guitar, 76, 77
  horn, 81
  piano, 77, 81
  saxophone, 81
  strings, 78
  tambourine, 77, 79–80
  triangles, 77
  trumpet, 81
  tuba, 81–82
  washboards, 77
  wind, 82, 83
inventions by African Americans
  gas mask, 11
  mailbox, 13
  railway signal, 11
Invisible Man (Ellison), 96

J

Jackson, Jesse, 7
Jackson, Mahalia, 77
Jackson Five, 78

"Jailhouse Rock", 77
Jamaica, 19, 84–85, 102
  food of, 102
jazz, 81–83
  passing the torch, 82
"Jazz Ahead", 82
Jazz Messengers, 82
jerk chicken, as Caribbean cuisine, 102
Jet magazine, 97
jigging, 88, 109
Joffrey Ballet, 89
Johnson, James Weldon, 96
Johnson, John H., 97
Johnson, Lyndon B., 7
Jones, James Earl, 95
Jones, Leroi. *See* Baraka, Amiri
Jones, Quincy, 75
jook joint, 75, 109
Joplin, Scott, 81
journal, making a, 98–99
jubilee, 77, 109
Juneteenth, 4, 14–17
  picnic basket for, 16–17
  reason for, 15
  rediscovering, 15
  tradition, 17

K

karamu, 19–20, 109
Karenga, Maulana Ron, 18, 20
Katherine Dunham Dance Company, 89
kei, 59
Kennedy, John F., 6
Kenya, 46
kettledrums, 55, 110
kikombe cha umoja, 19, 110
kinara, 19, 110
King, B. B., 77
King, Coretta Scott, 7
King, Dexter, 7
King, Denise, 7
King, Martin Luther Jr., 5–9
  Civil Rights movement and, 6–7
  honoring birthday of, 7
  "I Have a Dream" speech, 6
  scroll commemorating his contributions, 8–9
King, Martin Luther III, 7
King, Yolanda, 7
Kirkland, Debbie, 25
Kolese style of hair braiding, 34
Kool Herc, 85
Koroba style of hair braiding, 34
Kujichagulia, 19, 110
Kuumba, 19, 110
Kwanzaa, 4, 18–21, 110
  candles of, 19
  principles of, 19
  traditional Swahili greeting for, 20

L

Lesotho, 59, 66
Liberia, 50
Lincoln, Abraham, 15
literature, 95–99
  Harlem Renaissance works, 96
  magazines, 97
  newspapers, 97
  playwriting, 98
  poetry, 95–96
  slave narratives, 96
  women writers, 98
Little Rock, Arkansas, 13
Little Sally Walker, 64–65
LL Cool J, 85
Louisiana, 76, 81
lunch-counter sit-ins, 6

M

macaroni and cheese, as soul food, 102
magazines, African American/African American-owned, 98
  Black Enterprise, 97
  Crisis, 97
  Ebony, 97
  Ebony Man, 97
  Essence, 97
  Jet, 97
  Negro Digest, 97
  O, 97
mancala, 61–63, 110
  making the board, 62
mango, as centerpiece to Caribbean cuisine, 107
mankuntu, 55, 110
Marley, Bob, 84
Marsalis, Wynton, 82
Martin Luther King Jr. Day, 4, 5–9
masabe, 55, 110
mask making, 50–53
  faces of, 51
  origin materials, 50
  symbols of, 50–51, 53
  tradition, 53
  tribal, 51–52
Mattox, Thelma, 35, 37
mazao, 19, 110
McKay, Claude, 96
Melvin, Harold, and the Blue Notes, 78
Memphis, Tennessee, 81
"Memphis Blues, The", 76
Mesopotamia, 79
Mingus, Charles, 81
miniature quilt, 37–39
minstrel shows, 88, 110
mishumaa, 19, 110
Mississippi Delta, 76
Mitchell, Arthur, 87, 88, 89, 90,
Mitchell, Deborah, 87
mixing technique, 85
mkeka, 19, 110
Monk, Thelonious, 81
Montgomery (Alabama) bus boycott, 6, 12
Morgan, Garrett A., 11
Morrison, Toni, 98
Morton, Jelly Roll, 81
Motown, 78

muhindi, 19, 110
muraburaba, 59, 66–68, 110
music, 75–86
  blues, 75, 76–77
  gospel, 76–77
  jazz, 81–83
  rap, 75, 84–86
  soul, 76–78
musical game, 64–65
musimbo, 55, 110
muslin, 36, 110
mustard greens, as soul food,
  102
Myers, Walter Dean, 95

N

National Association for the
  Advancement of Colored
  People (NAACP), 97
National Book Award, 98
necklace for Kwanzaa, 20–
  21
Negro Digest, 97
Negro History Week, 11
New Jersey Tap Ensemble,
  87
New Orleans, Louisiana, 76,
  81

newspapers, African
  American, 97
  Amsterdam News, 97
  Freedom's Journal, 97
  Philadelphia Tribune, 97
Nguzo Saba, 18–19, 110
Nia, 19, 110
Nicholas Brothers, the,
  92
Nigeria
  calabash in, 43
  drums in, 55
  masks in, 50
  tie-dyeing in, 46, 49
Nobel Peace Prize, 7
Nobel Prize for Literature,
  98
North America, tambourine
  in, 79
Not without Laughter
  (Hughes), 96

O

Of Mules and Men
  (Hurston), 24
O'Jays, 78
O magazine, 97
owari. *See* mancala

P

papaya, as centerpiece to
  Caribbean cuisine, 107
Parker, Charlie, 81
Parks, Rosa, 6
patchwork, 35, 110
"Peculiar Such Thing, The",
  29
"People Could Fly, The",
  29
Philadelphia Tribune, 97
Pickett, Wilson, 78
picnic baskets for
  Juneteenth, 16–17
pilgrimage, 17, 110
pineapple, as centerpiece to
  Caribbean cuisine, 107
plantain, 102, 107–8
  fried, 107–8
playwriting, 98
poetry, 95–96
pone. *See* corn bread
pork, in soul food, 102
positions in ballet, 90–92
potato salad, as soul food,
  102
Powell, Bud, 81

Powers, Harriet, 36
"Precious Lord, Take My
  Hand", 77
Presley, Elvis, 77
Pulitzer Prize, 98

Q

quilting, 35–40, 110
  appliqué technique, 40, 109
  history of, 36
  making a miniature, 37–39
  message in, 36
  tradition, 40
quilts, names of patterns,
  36–37
  "Pineapple", 36
  "Rising Sun", 36
  "Sawtooth", 36
  "Triangles", 37
  "Wedding Ring", 36

R

race records, 77, 110
ragtime, 81
Rainey, Ma, 76
rap, 75, 84–86
  writing, 85–86
Ray, James Earl, 7

Reagan, Ronald, 7
recipes
  biscuits, 105–6
  corn bread, 104–5
Redding, Otis, 78
red snapper, as Caribbean
    cuisine, 102
"Respect", 78
reggae, 84
"Revelations", 89
rhythm and blues. *See* soul
Robinson, Bill "Bojangles",
    92
rock steady style of music, 84
Rooks, Noliwe M., 30
Run-D.M.C., 85
Russwurm, John B. 97

S

salt fish, as Caribbean
    cuisine, 102
Sam and Dave, 78
sampling, musical definition
    of, 84, 110
"Say It Loud, I'm Black and
    I'm Proud", 78
scroll, for Martin Luther
    King Jr., 8–9

seega, 59
"Shake It to the One That
    You Love the Best", 65
shoes, tap, 93–94
Shook, Karel, 89
shuffle step, of tap, 92
Sierra Leone, 59
Simms, Howard "Sandman",
    92
sit-ins, lunch-counter, 6
ska, 84
slave
  celebrations, 3–4, 15
    folktales, 23, 26
  food of, 102
  music of, 75–76, 77
  quilts and, 35
slave narratives, 96, 110
slap step, of tap, 92
Smith, Bessie, 76
Smith, Jennie, 36
Smithsonian Institution, 15
Smithsonian's National
    Museum of American
    History, 36
Sophisticated Ladies, 93
soul food, 19, 101–2, 105
  for Kwanzaa, 19

tradition, 105
soul music, 76–78
Souls of Black Folk, The, 96
"sound of Philadelphia"
    music style, 78
South Africa, 66
"Stack-Up, The", 89
stamp step, of tap, 92
Staple Singers, 78
"St. Louis Blues", 76
storytelling, 25–29, 36
  through quilts, 36
Sugar Hill Gang, 85
Suku style of hair braiding,
    34
Supremes, the, 78
Swahili
  names of Nguzo Saba (prin-
    ciples of Kwanzaa), 19
  greeting, 20
sweet potato pie, as soul
    food, 19, 102
swing, style of music, 81
syncopated, 84, 111

T

talking drum, making, 56–57
tall tale, 26–27

tambourine, 79–80, 111
  making, 79–80
Tanzania, 46
Tap, 93
tap dancing, 88–94, 111
  shoes, making, 93–94
  steps of, 92
taro root leaves, as center-
    piece to Caribbean
    cuisine, 107
Tatum, Art, 81
Temple, Shirley, 92
Temptations, The, 78
*Their Eyes Were Watching
    God* (Hurston), 96
thumping sticks. *See* Chigoro
    Danda
tie-dyeing (adire), 46–49
  tradition, 49
time step, of tap, 92
Tindley, Charles A., 77
toasting, definition of
    Jamaican term, 85
Toomer, Jean, 96
tradition (specific)
  surrounding
    hair-braiding, 34
    Juneteenth, 17

Kwanzaa, 20
mask making, 53
quilting, 40
soul food, 105
storytelling, 29
tap dancing, 94
tie-dye, 49
traditions, African
    American, 23–40
  hair braiding, 30–34
  quilting, 35–40
  storytelling, 25–29
triangles as musical
    instruments, 77
tribal mask, making, 51–53
Trinidad, food of, 102
tropical fruits, as center-
    pieces to Caribbean
    cuisine, 107
T-shirt, tie-dyeing, 47–49

Tubman, Harriet, 11
turnip, as soul food, 102

U

Ujama, 19, 111
Ujima, 19, 111
Umoja, 19, 111
United States Supreme
    Court, 6, 13
unity cup, 19, 110, 111

V

vaudeville, 76–77, 88, 92,
    111
Vaughan, Sarah, 81
Voting Rights Act of 1965,
    7

W

Wailers, the, 84
Walker, Alice, 98

Walker, Madam C. J., 11
Wallace, George, 6
wari. *See* mancala
washboard as musical
    instrument, 77
Waters, Muddy, 77
Weary Blues, The (Hughes),
    96
Weidman, Charles, 88
"We Shall Overcome", 77
West Africa
  games in, 61
  quilt making, 36, 40
  tie-dyeing, 46
Wheatley, Phyllis, 95–96
White, Barry, 78
wind instrument, making,
    83
Winfrey, Oprah, 97

"Wolf and Little Daughter,
    The", 26–27
Wonder, Stevie, 7, 78
Woodson, Carter G., 11
Wright, Richard, 96

Y

Yoruba
  language, 55
  names for cornrow styles,
    34
Yote, 59

Z

Zaire, 55. *See also* Congo
Zambia, drums in, 55
zawadi, 20, 111
Zimbabwe, games in, 60, 64,
    69